PLAYING OUTDOORS

Debating Play Series

Series Editor: Tina Bruce, Honorary Visiting Professor at Roehampton University, London

The intention behind the 'Debating Play' series is to encourage readers to reflect on their practices so that they are in a position to offer high quality play opportunities to children. The series will help those working with young children and their families, in diverse ways and contexts, to think about how to cultivate early childhood play with rich learning potential.

The 'Debating Play' series examines cultural myths and taboos. It considers matters of human rights and progress towards inclusion in the right to play for children with complex needs. It looks at time-honoured practices and argues for the removal of constraints on emergent play. It challenges readers to be committed to promoting play opportunities for children traumatized by war, flight, violence and separation from loved ones. The series draws upon crucial contemporary research which demonstrates how children in different parts of the world develop their own play culture in ways which help them make sense of their lives.

Published and forthcoming titles

Forbes: *Beginning to Play*
Holland: *We Don't Play With Guns Here*
Hyder: *War, Conflict and Play*
Kalliala: *Play Culture in a Changing World*
Manning-Morton and Thorp: *Key Times for Play*
Orr: *My Right to Play: A Child with Complex Needs*

PLAYING OUTDOORS

SPACES AND PLACES, RISK AND CHALLENGE

Helen Tovey

Open University Press

Open University Press
McGraw-Hill Education
McGraw-Hill House
Shoppenhangers Road
Maidenhead
Berkshire
England
SL6 2QL

email: enquiries@openup.co.uk
world wide web: www.openup.co.uk

and

Two Penn Plaza, New York, NY 10121-2289, USA

First published 2007

A catalogue record of this book is available from the British Library

ISBN10: 0 335 21641 2 (pb)   0 335 21643 9 (hb)
ISBN13: 978 0 335 21641 3 (pb)   978 0 335 21643 7 (hb)

Library of Congress Cataloging-in-Publication Data
CIP data has been applied for

Typeset by RefineCatch Limited, Bungay, Suffolk
Printed in Great Britain by Bell and Bain Ltd., Glasgow

CONTENTS

SERIES EDITOR'S PREFACE

Friedrich Froebel emphasised the importance of the garden and the educational importance of learning out of doors more than a century ago. It is therefore appropriate that a modern day Froebelian should write about the way children nowadays can be supported and extended in learning of this kind.

Helen Tovey, who is a Principal Lecturer based in the Froebel College at Roehampton University, has brought together important strands in what it means to learn out of doors in this timely book. There is great concern amongst those working with and spending time with children that there is still too much emphasis on learning indoors. Despite efforts to legally enshrine the requirement for children to be offered rich opportunities to learn outdoors, this has not yet happened.

It is the enduring spirit of the Froebelian emphasis on learning out of doors which is important. Determined practitioners of all kinds have always given it a priority and a high place in the way they have developed learning environments of quality. The Maintained Nursery Schools, pioneered by the Froebelian Margaret McMillan at the turn of the century have been shining examples and leaders in this, and their excellence continues to be reflected in Ofsted reports, praising their use of outdoor experiences in the quality of what they offer young children. Many of the Maintained Nursery Schools are transforming into Children's Centres, keeping the emphasis on learning out of doors.

This book will give support and encouragement to practitioners working with other people's children to offer high quality experiences of learning out of doors in rich and varied ways. It gives theoretical insights into why this is important, and builds on time-honoured historic traditions encouraging practice that is effective and current.

Professor Tina Bruce
Roehampton University

ACKNOWLEDGEMENTS

This book grew from discussions on outdoor play with Pat Gura and Pauline Boorman—many years ago but still vibrant and memorable today.

Many people have helped me develop the ideas and images. Particular thanks to Sally Pointer, Louisa Halls, Norma Frood, Kath Robinson, Olivia Peake, Diane Ward, Katherine Milchem, and the staff and children at Somerset Nursery School, Bridgwater College Children's Centre, Guildford Children's Centre, Lanterns Children's Centre, Oxfordshire Forest School and Redford House Nursery, Roehampton University.

I am grateful to Ingunn Fjortoft for allowing me to include her photos of Norwegian nature kindergartens (Figures 5.5 and 5.8) and to Elaine Keating for her photos of Oxfordshire forest schools (Figures 5.2, 5.3, 5.4). Thanks for photos also to Alex Cole and Laura Johnson for Figure 5.1, Norma Frood for Figure 4.7 and Guildford Children's Centre for Figure 6.1.

Special thanks to all my colleagues at the Early Childhood Research Centre at Roehampton University, and particularly to Peter Elfer, Sue Greenfield, Shirley Maxwell and Fengling Tan for critical feedback on draft chapters and to Lisa Guy for help with literature searches. I am especially grateful to the series editor, Tina Bruce for her patience, positive encouragement and timely sternness without which I might still be writing.

Love and gratitude to my partner, Senaka Jayasinghe for steady support, technical troubleshooting and for his fine cooking, which sustained me through long days and nights of writing.

Finally for a childhood full of open spaces, secret places and risky, challenging play, I'm forever grateful to my parents, Nesta and Douglas Tovey.

1

CHILDREN'S LIVES

Think about your own childhood play. Where did you play and what did you do? If you are over 30 years old the chances are that you played outdoors in gardens, streets, alleys, woods, fields, orchards, bomb sites, waste ground, in between spaces and secret places. The likelihood is that you got very dirty and were intimately involved with nature whether climbing trees, finding tadpoles or building a den in bushes. Consider this memory from Tim Smidt, Chief Executive of the Eden Project:

> My childhood was rich in smells, noises, warmth and little frissons of terror—mostly of my own making. I climbed trees with daring but was hugely frightened. I lifted stones wherever I went in order to inhale the smell of moist earth and the slightly lemony smell of crushed bracken. My thrills were slow worms and toads. There was pond dipping and racing water boatmen, catching sticklebacks and grazing my knees falling off bicycles and out of trees. . . . Often I took my shoes off and loved the tickly feeling of cut grass, the swishy feeling of long grass, the irresistible roughness of hard sand the exotic caress of dry sand; but most of all there was mud. How glorious to let it squidge through your toes! And peeling it off when it dried was another sensation altogether.
>
> (Smidt, cited in Rich *et al* 2005: 6)

The opportunity to experience such joyful, sensory rich, adventurous play is severely limited for many children growing up today and arguably has never been available for children living in poverty in inner city areas. Pioneers of early childhood education, such as Margaret

McMillan, have long campaigned for the provision of nursery gardens for children living in overcrowded squalid conditions or in bleak, concrete inner city estates. Poverty has shaped the experiences of children's play outdoors and continues to do so today. Children growing up in poverty are more likely to be in overcrowded accommodation, more likely to be marginalized from both public and private play spaces, less likely to access green spaces such as gardens and, at the same time, are more exposed to the dangers of traffic and, therefore, more prone to road traffic accidents (Greater London Authority 2004).

Decline in freedom to play outdoors

The freedom to play outdoors is declining rapidly for many children living in both urban and rural areas. Research on children's independent mobility, the area around the home to which children can roam, suggests that it has shrunk to a ninth of what it was in the 1970s. Ten-year-olds have a much smaller and more clearly specified area in which they can play freely, are monitored much more by parents and are likely to have their play curtailed at any hint of danger (Hillman *et al* 1990). Increase in traffic has made most local streets unsafe as places for play and the car, which has brought such benefits in broadening children's experiences of spaces further afield, has severely restricted children's freedoms to become really acquainted with their own local spaces.

The decline in waste ground once favoured play spaces of older children has also contributed to the lack of play outdoors. It is now twenty years since Robin Moore's (1986) classic study of three contrasting urban neighbourhoods in England and his meticulous documentation of children's spaces and places for play. It is salutary to reflect on how, in such a short space of time, favourite places such as streets, fences, footpaths, parks, open spaces and waste ground have all but disappeared or are now effectively out of bounds for children.

Culture of fear

The decline in access to outdoor spaces for play has been paralleled by an unprecedented rise in the level of anxiety for children's safety, a 'culture of fear' (Furedi 2002). It appears that parental anxiety and fear of child abduction or 'stranger danger' has had the most pervasive effect on children's play (Valentine and McKendrick 1997). Surveys of parents reveal that very few would let their children play out unsupervised, and children themselves place fear of abduction or murder at the top of their concerns about play outdoors (Lindon 1999; Gill 2006a,b). Yet, paradoxically, children have never been safer, and incidents of child abduction and murder, although tragic, are extremely rare and have remained largely unchanged in the last fifty years. It is the fear of danger that has contributed to a decline in children's freedom to play outdoors, placing them at greater risk from accident or abuse within the home.

Over-organized lives

Admission to primary school at a younger age, and the rapid growth of nursery, child care and after school care means that young children's lives are increasingly institutionalized. Out of school care is often located in school environments, under close adult supervision with, in many settings, organized activities replacing free play. The growth in after school activities, such as clubs, sports, or extra lessons, can mean that many children's leisure time is increasingly structured and organized by adults with less time for children to initiate their own play. The length of playtime in many primary schools has been reduced amid concerns about children's behaviour and opportunities for play are limited by the pressures of a centralized curriculum. Jenkinson (2001: 14) refers to 'wrapped around play', that is play that is shaped and directed by adults, and becomes 'wrapped around' a focused learning objective. Polakow (1992: 62) identifies a kind of play that she calls 'controlled play', that is play that is over-managed and curtailed by cautious adults.

Time pressures and fears for children's safety contribute to children being transported to nurseries in push chairs when they are well able to walk or escorted to school when they are able to travel alone. The numbers of seven- and eight-year-old children who travel to school on their own has dropped from 80 per cent in 1971 to 10 per cent in 1990 (Hillman *et al* 1990) and I suspect has fallen further still today. The huge increase in numbers of children driven to school by car paradoxically makes the streets around schools less safe and more polluted. Children also lose some autonomy, as well as the opportunity to learn the skills of being a pedestrian, of negotiating public transport, or of walking, talking and playing with their peers or parents on short journeys around their neighbourhood. Risotto and Giuliani (2006) reviewed research that suggests that children who walk to school have more developed spatial skills and more knowledge of the social fabric of the neighbourhood than those driven to school, indicating that navigating local streets has an impact on cognition, as well as a developing a sense of belonging in a place.

Local streets, taken at a slow pace, become places of wonder and discovery to a young child. Alison Gopnik suggests that taking a walk with a toddler is like taking a walk with William Blake:

> There are gates, gates that open one way and not another and that will swing back and forth if you push them just the right way. There are small walls you can walk on very carefully. There are sewer lids that have fascinating regular patterns and scraps of brightly coloured pizza–delivery flyers. There are intriguing strangers to examine carefully from behind a protective parental leg. There is a veritable zoo of creatures, from tiny pill bugs and earthworms to the enormous excitement, or terror, of a real barking dog.
>
> (Gopnik *et al* 1999: 211)

Increase in car travel has opened up new spaces for children, but at the same time separates children from the outside world and such everyday adventures. Children are cocooned in an artificially conditioned inside environment despite being 'outside' their homes. The growing trend for seat-back screen-based entertainment means that there is little need for children to create their own entertainment or even to engage with the wider world outside the window. Cars have taken away children's freedom to play in many local streets close to home amid justifiable fear of accident. The local street has traditionally been an important social space for children to meet and play, often in mixed age groups and close enough to home to be freely accessible and to feel safe.

Growing intolerance of children's play

There is also some evidence of a growing intolerance to children's play outdoors. A nursery in Cornwall, for example, was required to reduce by half the time children spent outdoors because of complaints of noise from local residents (Fox 2005). In Surrey a play centre was closed because of complaints about the noise (Gibbs 2005) and a survey by The Children's Society found numerous examples of children who had been stopped from playing because of 'grumpy adults' (The Children's Society 2003). There is, maybe, nothing new in this. There has always been some intolerance of children's play as Iona and Peter Opie have identified:

> In the nineteenth century there were repeated complaints that the pavements of London were made impassable by children's

shuttlecock and tipcat. In Stuart times, Richard Steele reported, the vicinity of the Royal Exchange was infested with uninvited sportsmen, and a beadle was employed to whip away the 'unlucky Boys with Toys and Balls'. . . . In 1332 it was found necessary to prohibit boys and others from playing in the precincts of the Palace of Westminster while Parliament was sitting. In 1385 the Bishop of London was forced to declaim against the ball-play about St Paul's.

(Opie and Opie 1969: 11)

The difference today is that play in contemporary urban areas has largely disappeared from residential streets. However, small but growing initiatives such as 'Home Zones', where streets are designed to be accessible to all users including children, are providing some evidence that children are returning to local streets as places to play (Gill 2006a,b).

Lack of space—out of place

Children, it seems are increasingly 'out of place' in many of our cities. Helen Penn argues that 'one of the most significant changes in the urban landscape over the last century has been the disappearance of children . . . Like the sky lark they have become endangered' (Penn 2005a: 180). This is not such an exaggerated claim when you look for yourself for evidence of children playing unsupervised in open, green or communal spaces. In my experience, there are many more dogs and owners enjoying such spaces than children. Where they do play out, unaccompanied children can be viewed with some suspicion and be seen as a potential nuisance, or even worse as potential criminals. Parents who wish to give their children freedom to play can be perceived as irresponsible and lacking in appropriate care.

Virtual spaces

It seems ironic that, while children explore and navigate shrinking amounts of 'real space', they can explore and navigate infinite amounts of 'virtual space'. Television and the rapid growth in screen-based electronic games provides a seductive alternative to playing outside and children can enter into dynamic and exciting fantasy worlds without having to move from their seats. Real world thrills, excitement and risk are replaced by their electronic equivalents. However, there are very real differences; the electronic world is two-dimensional, provides limited sensory feedback, and is usually solitary and sedentary. It can offer an exciting escape from real life, but is no substitute for it. Of course, increasingly sophisticated technology is part of all children's lives and offers huge benefits. The issue is more that as with any rapid social change we have to reflect on how appropriate excessive consumption of electronic entertainment is in early childhood when children are growing rapidly and require a diverse, rather than a restricted range of new experiences. The time spent watching screens can take away from the time spent actively engaging with people and things and excessive watching can impact on children's learning, health and well being:

For the first time in the 4 million year history of our species, we are effectively trapping children indoors at the very point when their bodies and minds are primed to start getting to grips with the world outside the home.

(Gill 2004)

Health

Childhood obesity has increased dramatically in the last twenty years. Statistics commissioned by the Department of Health indicate that nearly 30 per cent of children aged two to ten were identified as overweight or obese in 2006. Children from poor families and those living in inner city areas are at greater risk of obesity than those from more affluent families or living in suburban or rural areas (Department of Health 2006). Research in Scotland indicates that today's three-year-olds weigh more than their counterparts twenty-five years ago and that pre-school children without spaces to play can be as inactive as office workers (Reilly *et al* 2003). Habits persist and overweight children are more likely to become overweight adults. Overweight and obesity are linked with chronic health problems, such as type 2 diabetes and potential cardiovascular disease, as well as psychological and social factors such as poor self-esteem, lack of confidence and social discrimination in friendship choices (British Medical Association 2005; Underdown 2007).

While the causes of overweight and obesity are complex there is little doubt that the 'obesogenic' environment with a loss of opportunity for spontaneous and vigorous outdoor play is one significant contributory factor. Indeed, a Report by the International Obesity Task Force (IOTF) in Europe urged governments to move away from what was argued to be ineffective 'health education' and to focus instead on the current 'toxic environment' including lack of outdoor play space. Children, they argue 'deserve to be given back the freedom to play and exercise in safety enjoyed by previous generations' (IOTF 2002: 28).

In the growing panic about rising levels of obesity and numbers of overweight children, it is important that we expand the range and opportunities for self-motivated and challenging play outdoors, rather than introduce indoor didactic 'exercise' sessions or such things as exercise bicycles in nurseries. The director of the firm marketing these to nurseries and primary schools is quoted as saying 'inner-city schools can use the equipment to compensate for limited outdoor space' (Bloom 2006). Yet it is hard to see how a stationery exercise bicycle can replace outdoor play. Movement is part of children's very being, and it is play and exploration that motivate children to move, not 'keeping fit'. Installing treadmills for toddlers is not the answer. Instead, in the words of a leading authority on childhood obesity writing in the *British Medical Journal*, 'opportunities for spontaneous play may be the only requirement that young children need to increase their physical activity' (Dietz 2001).

Outdoor play impacts on mental as well as physical health and a report from the Mental Health Foundation (1999) stated that the lack of opportunities for play outdoors contributes to mental health problems in children and families, especially where there are already existing stresses. Social housing in cities can add to the problem and children living in high rise flats have no easy access to outdoor space. An active toddler and a depressed, socially-isolated mother can be a toxic mix for both parent and child. Play outdoors develops friendships, reduces social isolation and gives children a sense of autonomy and control, all important features of mental and physical well being.

Where do children play outdoors?

While the amount of public space for children's play has declined the amount of private and commercially run play spaces in shopping malls, gardens of pubs and restaurants, leisure centres, and theme parks has increased dramatically. These are often indoors offering 'safe' environments, such as 'soft play' materials. They generally offer a commercially-focused, often standardized, adult-centred view of play. Provision can be fun and entertaining, but no substitute for rich and sustained free play. This type of play provision is clearly less likely to be accessible to children growing up in poverty, estimated to be about 29 per cent across England rising to 54 per cent in Inner London (Greater London Authority 2004).

Nursery and school settings

Given the decline of safe, free, easily accessible play spaces for young children, institutional settings, such as schools, nurseries, day care and out-of-school care are increasingly important in providing space where young children can play with friends on a regular basis. However, while some settings provide opportunities for exciting, inspiring and challenging outdoor play, the quality of provision can be variable.

At the time of writing there are no national standards for outdoor space for early years provision in the UK in contrast to many other European countries. It is therefore possible for nurseries to operate with little or even no outdoor space. It is somewhat ironic that some local authorities have regulations requiring parking space for cars, but not play space for children with the result that cars can take precedence over children in the battle for scarce resources. It is also ironic that free-range organic chickens are required by law to have year round access to a minimum of 4 square metres of grassy space, yet it is acceptable for some young children to be battery-reared for large parts of the day and year without ever seeing a patch of sky or blade of grass. It is relevant to note that England has one of the lowest indoor space requirements in Europe, currently 3.5 square metres for every child under two and 2.3 square metres for every child aged three to five (Children in Europe 2005). This suggests that space for movement and activity, so important for growing children, can be restricted both indoors and outdoors. While national standards are not always the best way to improve provision, nevertheless, the absence of any requirement for outdoor provision for young children communicates an important symbolic message about the value of play outdoors.

I visited one nursery that had no outdoor provision at all. Instead, physical play was timetabled to take place in a basement room with no natural light or fresh air. Here, children from two to five spent up to nine hours a day. Where outdoor space is available, its quality can be poor. Space can be flat, cage-like, covered in rubber surfacing, with a sprinkling of plastic toys, devoid of sensory stimulation, discovery, adventure, and bearing little relation at all to what we know about young children's learning and development.

Outdoor play for four-year-old children in primary school reception classes can also be problematic and a large research project on reception classes in England (Adams *et al* 2004), commissioned by the Association of Teachers and Lectures, found that provision of an appropriate outdoor learning environment was very variable, with some children experiencing only a bare concrete playground. Free movement between indoors and outdoors was often constrained and curtailed. Research on early years settings in primary schools in Wales (Maynard and Waters 2006) found that teachers' underpinning rationale for the use of the outdoors was often ill-defined and vague. Although reference to 'freedom' was cited, in practice teachers used the outdoors not for play at all but for a series of goal-directed tasks or whole class teaching. For example, in one reception class the teacher took a mat outside for all the children to sit on in order to carry out a sorting task. As a result, many of the opportunities that the outdoor area afforded for play were missed. Teachers also identified many difficulties such as access to play areas, storage of equipment, staffing and supervision, suggesting that there were wider structural issues that impeded the development of play outdoors.

In 1989 the Department for Education and Science surveyed the quality of provision for four-year-olds in primary schools and concluded that 'four year olds rarely had opportunity for outdoor activities'. This, the report argued, was partly due to resourcing difficulties, but more significantly because 'in most cases the value of outdoor play and the contribution it can make were not well understood' (HMI 1989: 7)

This would seem to be the crux of the issue. Despite the much higher profile given to outdoor play in recent years with the introduction of the Curriculum Guidance for the Foundation Stage (QCA 2000), there is still evidence that the 'purpose and value of outdoor play is not well understood'. Paradoxically, the provision of challenging outdoor play has long been a distinctive feature of the early childhood tradition with the pioneers of early childhood education, such as Friedrich Froebel, Maria Montessori, Margaret McMillan, Rudolph Steiner and Susan Isaacs, advocating outdoor provision as essential for children's learning and development.

Decline in independent mobility of children, anxiety about children's safety, the growing institutionalization of children's lives, have all contributed to a rising tide of concern about the nature of childhood today. Polakow (1992) warned many years ago about the growing 'containment of childhood'. Palmer (2006) refers to the lack of opportunity for play outdoors as one ingredient in a 'toxic childhood' and the UK Children's Society is taking evidence on 'what makes a good childhood'. I would argue that regular, challenging play outdoors is an essential part of a good childhood and, indeed a fundamental right. This is an issue that involves policy makers, planners and landscape architects, as well as early childhood practitioners but underpinning any change has to be an understanding of the purpose and value of outdoor play and it is this we consider in Chapter 2.

The landscapes we create are powerful testament to how we as a culture treat the natural world. If we asphalt the entire play yard, surround it with chain link fence and fill it with plastic toys and organized sports what does that tell children?

(Herrington 2005a: 216)

2

WHY OUTDOOR PLAY?

Underpinning values

Why is play outdoors important? Too often attention focuses on 'how' without addressing the more fundamental 'why'? Yet, without the answers to such a question, outdoor provision and practice lacks any coherent rationale and is likely to reflect uncritical assumptions about young children, and their play and learning. Underpinning all outdoor settings there are values. Consider the very different values that underpin these three nursery settings for three- and four-year-old children.

Setting 1

The doors open at 11.00 a.m. and all the children are required to go outside. For twenty minutes most children pedal round the yard on individual bikes skilfully avoiding each other. There is little inter-action though many vocalizations. One adult supervises the play-ground trying in vain to interest those children who do not have a bike. Meanwhile, the adults indoors clear up, set the tables for dinner and make coffee. At 11.20 a.m. the children are required to park their bikes and line up to come indoors. This takes considerable time as some children are reluctant to part with their bikes having only just managed to achieve a turn. At 11.30 a.m. precisely the doors are opened and the children, many fractious and argumentative, are required to listen to a story.

Setting 2

It is a fine day, and the outdoor area has been filled with tables and equipment brought from indoors. Children sit at tables with activities such as colour matching games and drawing. The thick wax crayons are beginning to melt in the sun providing some interest. One group of children is sitting on a mat sorting shapes with an adult. Another group is more active, throwing different coloured bean bags into different coloured tubs. One group plays in the small wooden house. 'That's blue group's turn' I was told by a four-year-old girl. 'When it's red group it will be my turn'.

Setting 3

The doors are wide open and children free to move between indoors and outdoors. A group of children are knee deep in the sand pit digging channels for water to flow along. There is much excitement as the water floods over the channel and they need to dig deeper. Other children are operating a pulley to transport water to the sand pit. A group of boys are rolling down a grass bank inside a barrel; they are trying to work out how to make the barrel roll straight. On the grass an elaborate drama unfolds as children build a jeep out of crates, tyres and planks and then set off on safari in search of imaginary animals. An adult and a group of children are totally engrossed in investigating worms and insects as they dig a patch of garden.

Implicit within these three settings are very different values about the purpose of the outdoor area. Setting 1 claimed to have 'well resourced and stimulating outdoor play', but in practice the space was used for children to race round and let off steam. The space was a convenient place for children to go while adults did something else. The status of play outdoors was diminished in the eyes of both children and adults. It is all too easy to draw on this recreational module of play as it is what many of us have experienced in our own schooling.

In setting 2 the outdoors was seen as a place to use in good weather only. It replicates what is available indoors, rather than exploiting the uniqueness of the outdoors. Implicit within the practice is a model of learning as broadly sedentary with a sharp divide between work, the tasks that children are required to do and play, what children get to do. Although the setting claims to have an attractive garden for play, in practice there is no spontaneous play, only adult-directed tasks. Play has been hijacked by adults for a narrowly conceived learning outcome. Adults remain firmly in control.

Setting 3, in contrast, is underpinned by values of choice and autonomy, challenge and risk. Within certain boundaries, children have
the freedom to determine their own activity with or without adults.
This environment reflects a belief in the value of direct first-hand
experience, and a model of play as freedom to pursue ideas, explore,
innovate, imagine and create. These are perceived as of central importance in all areas of children's development and learning. Health,
well being, physical, social, emotional and cognitive dimensions of
experience are integrated.

So why is outdoor play important?

A unique environment offering learning opportunities that are not available indoors

First, outdoors offers a unique environment, which is qualitatively different from indoors. It offers the space and a greater degree of freedom
to try things out, to explore and experiment without the constraints
associated with an indoor environment. Children therefore have more
scope to 'have a go' at something, without worrying about the consequences. Being willing to have a go at something is an important
learning disposition (Katz 1995). Space is more open, less confined and
the greater the space, the more expansive the movement possibilities.
Indoors is a space where adults are in control, but outdoors is perceived
as a child's domain where regulation is less, and where children can
escape the watchful and controlling eyes of adults (Stephenson 2002).
Outdoor space can literally 'free up' the body and the mind.

Play materials associated with indoors can be experienced on a
much larger scale outdoors, offering a substantially different experience. For example, children might experience a small plastic water
pump or water wheel in indoor water play, but outside they can
experience a large scale pump or water wheel offering a richer range of
experiences with more opportunities for collaboration and problem
solving (see Figure 2.1). Painting inside might happen on easels or
tables but outside can take place on many different surfaces with a
range of different materials. Painting with large brushes and water
enables children to cover large surfaces, to paint up high or down
low. This encourages free shoulder movements and the confidence to
make large bold movements which might not be possible indoors. In
this sense the outdoors can complement the indoors and children are
able to make connections in their learning. Making connections is
fundamental to children's learning (Athey 1990).

Resources that are usually kept separate indoors, such as construction play and water play can be more easily combined outdoors

Figure 2.1 Outdoors offers large-scale experiences which can complement those indoors.

offering a greater degree of challenge as the materials change and become more problematic. The more challenging the materials the more likely it is that children become involved sometimes spending many hours in constructing water ways and solving problems (see Figure 2.2). Laevers (cited in Pascal and Bertram 1997) suggests that it is when children are most involved that deep level learning takes place.

Figure 2.2 Construction and water play can more easily be combined outdoors.

Outdoors is a dynamic environment, which is always changing—the air, temperature, light, weather conditions, seasons are in constant flux. Puddles appear and disappear, clouds move, flower buds open, snails emerge after rain. The entire space transforms on a foggy day. Outdoors is full of unpredictability and the sheer variability of the outdoors as an environment is what makes it unique. An indoor environment, in contrast, is relatively static, change is deliberate.

Because outdoor space is more fluid, it has greater potential for being shaped by children, and by children and adults together. The space can be manipulated, equipment moved and materials moulded, giving children more control and a sense of agency. Such a pliable, yielding environment can be empowering for children who have little control in other spheres of their lives.

A dynamic, open environment invites many possibilities for movement and action, but it can lack the security and stability of a more enclosed indoor. As Stephenson (2002) noted, children tend to move to the more intimate, enclosed spaces indoors when they are upset or anxious. However, this is qualified by her observation that the outdoor environment did not offer physical seclusion, whereas Herrington (1997) notes how careful design of the outdoor landscape can provide the more intimate, encompassing or what she refers to as 'embracing' landscapes and this is explored further in Chapter 4.

Outdoors offers a rich landscape of sensory experiences that stimulates the whole body. The sweet smell of lilac, the dank, musty smell of Autumn leaves, the gentle rustle of wind through bamboo, the aromatic taste of newly-picked tomatoes, the granular feel of sand and the cold, viscous feel of fresh mud are just examples of the sensory experiences outdoors (Figure 2.3). Indoors, where air, temperature, sound, smell, texture, is regulated the sensory range is much more limited. It is the sharp contrast in sensory experience that can offer the burst of energy associated with going outside and the sensation of freedom from the more dulling effects of the indoor environment. Young children learn through their senses, and through movement and sensory experiences provide the essential first-hand experience of the world. We learn about a place by touching, feeling, seeing, smelling, hearing it and responding emotionally. The connection between our senses and emotions can remain powerfully evocative throughout our lives.

> You'll go where laurel crowns are won, but—will you e'er forget
> The scent of hawthorn in the sun, or bracken in the wet?
>
> (Kipling)

A rich context for play

Play is not static, but fluid evolving as it flows across time and through space. Traditional models of play define play by categories such as exploratory play, imaginative play, sociodramatic play, games with rules and so on. However, as Reifel and Yeatman (1993) point out, such categories tend to distort our understanding of play that rarely fits

Figure 2.3 The sweet smell of lilac is just one example of sensory experiences outdoors.

neatly into a category and is much more likely to flow from one to another. What starts as exploration of materials can quickly move into problem-solving, then into a game with rules, then back to problem-solving, then into imaginative play.

Outdoors, with its greater space and freedom of movement, is especially supportive of this play, which ebbs and flows, gaining new ideas and momentum from peers, available props and features of the landscape. Play gains complexity as plots evolve and 'thicken' as new sequences are added. For example, after visiting a parcel sorting office, a group of reception class children played wrapping parcels, which were then slid down the conveyer belt (a wooden slide), stamped in a make-do parcel office and subsequently 'delivered' to different people and places across the play area.

Many of the themes of children's play involve such things as travelling, going on holiday, moving house, shopping, going to a garden centre, delivering things, car and train crashes, transporting patients to hospital, rescuing people, and chasing robbers and 'bad guys'. All of these themes involve movement, and are not easy to sustain and develop indoors, but can gain impetus from the more open outdoor space. Space and movement allows children to be more active, to make more choices and for play to flow with fewer disruptions.

Rogers and Evans (2006) researching role play in three reception classes in South West England noted that play outdoors was often more sustained, and its social and narrative content was more complex than the play observed indoors. This was significant for both girls and boys. They concluded that:

> Outdoor play spaces enable children to create play spaces themselves and to exercise greater choice over materials, location and playmates. [They] encourage girls to take on more active roles and engage in more construction activities as part of their role play (such as building the perimeters of a house or hospital) and enable the boys' play to develop with fewer disruptions to those around them and with fewer instances of conflict with adults indoors
>
> (Rogers and Evans 2006: 23)

While it is not possible to say that imaginative play outdoors is necessarily richer or more complex than that indoors, the potential for children to create, innovate, imagine, to combine and transform materials outdoors is considerably enhanced by the more flexible, open and indeterminate nature of the outdoor environment.

Imaginative transformations

Outdoors offers considerable scope for children to act on their environment and to transform it. Transformations include using one object, place or gesture to stand for another. For example, children might use a traffic cone to stand for a witch's hat or a ladder for a lawn mower or they transform a space in the bushes into a den or a climbing frame into a castle. All of these transformations involve representational and symbolic thinking. Vygotsky (1978) argued that such play leads to higher level thinking because children are using objects symbolically. The act of transformation involves symbolic, abstract thinking.

Max, aged four, is using a ladder to represent a mower having recently seen the gardeners cut the grass (Figure 2.4). Vygotsky's theory would suggest that the ladder is a prop or 'pivot' that helps Max to detach and explore the meaning of mowers, that they cut, have to be moved around, make a noise and so on. He uses his previous experience of things that cut, move and make a noise to announce that he is 'razoring' the grass, creatively inventing a new word that makes sense. He sees the ladder, but acts as though it is a mower. The ladder does not look like a mower, but it allows the appropriate gestures to be made. In reality, things dictate what we have to do with them, a ladder is for climbing, but in play the situation is reversed and 'actions arise from ideas rather than things' (Vygotsky 1978: 70). Max, therefore, has to hold on to two concepts at the same time and all his actions, gestures, vocalizations, movements, language arise from an abstract idea. For this reason, Vygotsky argues that play leads development as it allows children to explore meaning and contributes to the development of abstract thought.

Figure 2.4 Outdoors offers rich opportunity for children to transform objects symbolically. This boy is using a ladder to stand for a mower and is 'razoring' the grass.

While children will transform objects indoors, the outdoor environment offers a much greater degree of open-endedness, allowing children to develop greater fluency in using objects symbolically. The plastic food and realistic play material now endemic in indoor home corners require little transformation or, indeed, imagination. A plastic fried egg remains a plastic fried egg, whereas a flower, a leaf or a stone can stand for a fried egg or anything else that a child wants it to be. Children decide and are therefore in control of, rather than responding to images and ideas.

Negotiating such transformations requires further skill. Children have to enter into an agreement with others, whether peers or adults. 'You know and I know that this is a leaf, but we are both pretending it's a fried egg'. This meeting of minds at an abstract level—agreeing, communicating and sustaining the pretence, negotiating the characters, the scripts and the plots of the play requires considerable planning and negotiation. Research by Trawick-Smith suggests that the complexity of children's negotiation and communication about their play, what he terms 'meta-play', increases substantially when children use open-ended materials such as can be found outdoors because the materials are ambiguous.

> The uses of realistic props do not require as much explanation or justification, do not demand the same level of agreement among players. The forms and functions of a shopping list or a grocery cart are obvious; no ongoing negotiations are needed about what these represent. In contrast, transforming a wooden rod into a fire hose requires some debate, since so many alternative symbolizations can be imagined.
>
> (Trawick Smith 1998a: 245)

Opportunities for risky play

Outdoor play offers challenges for children to try things out, to have a go and take risks in their learning. Stephenson (2002) identifies the outdoor environment as rich in opportunities for 'scary' experiences, which offer thrill, excitement and feelings of being on the borderline of out of control. Confidence, adventurousness, daring, delight in tackling the unknown, the ability to assess and manage risk, and to know how to be safe are important learning dispositions that contribute to strong, capable learners. The value of risky play outdoors is considered in more depth in Chapter 6 of this book.

Gleefulness, giddiness and fooling about

Laughter, gleefulness, whooping and shrieking with delight are characteristic of young children's play, and contribute to a sense of outdoors as a place of joy where children can be both literally and metaphorically 'giddy with glee'. Rolling down grassy slopes, collecting dry leaves and throwing them in the air, playing chase, hiding and jumping in and out of a large barrel, pretending to be a 'flying spoon' chasing a 'flying saucer' are just a few examples of the gleeful play that I have observed recently.

Sometimes the glee is contagious and ripples throughout a whole group, such as when a group of four-year-olds decided to 'play babies' in the sandpit, and there was much filling up of clothes with dry sand, waddling round the play space, bellies filled with sand and then 'borning' the babies with a flourishing deposit of sand. As children collapsed in the sand in a heap of giggles, the mirth was infectious, and was 'caught' and enjoyed by most of the children and adults in the area.

Spinning around a post, twirling round and round, hanging upside down on the climbing frame, playing roly-poly down a bank, are examples of what Caillois (2001) refers to as 'dizziness', the enjoyable sense of dizziness that occurs when children voluntarily 'shake for a moment the trustworthiness of perception and sensation, thus creating an enjoyable feeling of dizziness'. However, he argues 'dizziness is not just a physical sensation but a mental phenomenon too and can occur as outbursts of fooling around or as a desire to shake the order and disturb a fixed way of being' (Kalliala 2006: 22).

'Fooling around, shaking the order of things and disturbing a fixed way of being' is a characteristic of play outdoors where supervision is less and children have greater freedom to innovate and develop their own rules. Such playful nonsense can be found in the jokes of toddlers, for example, a pair of two-year-olds put gloves on their heads and laughed. They then put hats on their hands and laughed again. Such humour often involves incongruous images, absurdities, discrepant events and double meanings. It is important in developing social understanding and establishing bonds of friendship. 'Discovering how to share a sense of absurdity and pleasure in the comic incidents of life is an important step toward intimacy' (Dunn 1988: 168).

Of course, humour and nonsense play is not unique to outdoors and can be found in many contexts, but it often thrives outdoors, where there is greater freedom and where adults can be more open to playful romping. Humour and nonsense are part of a long tradition of children's outdoor play, a culture of street and playground, which has been passed from generation to generation, changed and modified along the way, and documented so meticulously by Iona and Peter Opie (1969). Many of these games require movement, whether clapping, stamping, circling, skipping, marching, chasing, or bouncing. Such play often challenges authority, pushes out boundaries of what is permissible, and combines ideas in new and original ways. For example, these five- and six-year-olds have adapted a dipping chant to decide who is 'it':

Child A Ip dip doo, the dog's done a poo
         Who stepped in it?
         It was you.
         Not because you're dirty, not because you're clean
         My Mum says you're the fairy queen
         Out you must go (*finger rests on Child B*)
Child B Ip dip doo, the chicken got the flu
         Who is sick?
         It is YOU

(Suantah 2005)

Here, the rhythm and rhyme of a traditional game is adapted to reflect contemporary issues, such as dog poo and bird flu. New words are inserted, but the rules of the rhyme are kept. Kalliala (2006) suggests that such games of chance are important ways of avoiding quarrels. If everybody agrees to relinquish some power and give way to the more impartial laws of chance, then conflict can be avoided and play can continue.

Children do not just play with things, they play with ideas and, as Garvey has pointed out, no sooner have they found out how something is meant to be, than it becomes fun to distort it, to turn it around, look at it from different angles (1991: 70). This love of 'violating the existing order of things' (Chukovsky 1968: 92) is very noticeably in outdoor play where children have more freedom and less surveillance by adults.

It seems that what superficially looks like clowning and fooling and of course can be enjoyed as just that, has far reaching significance in children's lives and learning. Jokes and humour, for example, are important in the development of intimacy and friendship (Dunn 1988). Humour and playfulness contribute to a shared culture of meaning and conversational exchange (Trevarthen 1995). Delight in rhythm and rhyme, and repetition fosters an understanding of the structures, rules, sounds and poetry of language (Crystal 1998). The power and the pleasure of nonsense rhyme and alliterative play with language may also be the key to literacy (Whitehead 1995).

Philip Pullman, children's author, makes a powerful case for 'fooling around':

> The most valuable attitude we can help children adopt—the one that among other things helps children to write and read with most fluency and effectiveness and enjoyment—I can best characterise by the word playful ... It begins with nursery rhymes and nonsense poems, with clapping games and finger play and simple songs and picture books. It goes on to consist of fooling about with the stuff the world is made of: with sounds, and with shapes and colours, and with clay and paper and wood and metal, and with language. Fooling about, playing with it, pushing it this way and that, turning it sideways, painting it different colours, looking at it from the back, putting one thing on top of another, asking silly questions, mixing things up, making absurd comparisons discovering unexpected similarities, making pretty patterns, and all the time saying 'supposing ... I wonder ... What if?'
>
> (Pullman 2005)

Indoors there can be a tendency for the atmosphere to be more serious, where excitement can be seen as something to be dissipated and children urged to calm down. Outdoors children can play with abandon.

Rough and tumble play

Playing with abandon can include rough play, such as rolling, tumbling and romping about. Known as 'rough and tumble play', it involves wrestling, grappling, kicking, tumbling, rolling on the ground and chasing (Smith 2005). Research suggests it begins in the early years and peaks at the end of the primary years, and is often played by boys, but occasionally girls. Players have to be able to signal 'this is play' (Bateson 1956) to indicate that the actions are mock combat and are not for real. Such play signals include exaggerated gestures, laughing and smiling, and are very different from the gestures and expressions used in real fighting, which involve clenched teeth, grimacing and fixed gazes. Smith's research suggests that adults are less skilful at reading these signals than children themselves, and are likely to interpret such play fighting as aggressive and to intervene to curtail it. Interestingly, it appears that women are more likely than men to identify a sample of play fighting as aggressive (Goldstein 1992), which may explain why early years practitioners can be ambivalent or even sometimes hostile to rough and tumble play.

However, it appears from research that such play is much more than just playing about, but is important for maintaining friendships and developing skills of communication, encoding and decoding signals. It involves self-restraint as players have to withhold the force that would lead, say, to a real kick, and take turns as they alternate who is 'on top' (Smith 2005). It also involves considerable camaraderie as children enjoy the close physical contact, the thrill of the chase and the conspiratorial enjoyment of doing things that are not what they seem to be.

A context for children's peer culture

Fooling around, playing rough and tumble are just some examples of children's own play culture, a culture that can, at times, appear as challenging to the adult culture. Such a culture contains many threads of the stories, events and images of the adult world, including the characters, plots and scripts of children's literature and popular media. These threads are reworked and woven into children's own play culture.

Such play outdoors involves a world of make believe, adventures, fights, chases, captures, rescues. Danger and the fear of danger can underpin much of the play and Corsaro (2003) in his ethnographic study of children's peer culture noted that tidal waves, earthquakes, falls from cliffs, fires, quicksand and poison were frequent themes in children's play—not the sort of themes that appear on adults' planning sheets. Practitioners on in-service courses report how bombs, explosives, train, bus and plane crashes feature in children's play outdoors since the events of 9/11. I have seen children playing versions of local gangland shootings and killings in a nursery school outdoor play area. Many of the themes of play are universal ones of the battle between good and evil, being lost and found, threat and averting a threat, birth, death and rebirth. Sometimes aspects of adult life, such as love, sex, jealousy and suicide, are incorporated into the play and Kalliala (2006) provides a powerful example of a dramatic enactment of 'suicide' on the playground slide by a group of six-year-old girls.

Such themes are not always viewed favourably by adults, who are sometimes reluctant to accept this darker side to children's play and expect children to play 'nicely', but the greater freedom, openness and space outdoors allow children the control to confront and examine such powerful and universal themes. As Goleman (1996) points out, magically changing the outcomes of the real world events can be powerful ways in which children gain some control over fear. At the same time, as in any subculture, the shared language, familiar narratives and enactments provide a strong sense of 'togetherness'. Corsaro (2003) suggests that the main themes in children's peer culture involve children trying to gain control of their lives and sharing that sense of control with each other.

Outdoors children can engage with the natural world and begin to understand their own place within it

> The world of nature is not a 'scene' or even a landscape. Nature for the child is sheer sensory experience.
>
> (Cobb 1977: 28)

Nature offers surprise, excites curiosity and invites exploration. The bean stem circling its way round a pole, the toad hiding in the drain, the seemingly ordinary things can be a source of fascination for children. Four-year-old Otis loved to fill up the bag of nuts on the bird table in the nursery garden. He drew a picture of the bird table with the bag of nuts from the outside and another view from the inside (Figure 2.5a). However, he was puzzled about where the nuts went and why the bag was empty. Where have all the nuts gone? We can see his puzzlement and his 'possibility thinking' in his second drawing (Figure 2.5b), maybe the nuts are now inside the bird and that is why the bag is empty! He represents his experiences graphically, but there are elements of creative thinking—'just suppose, what if?' As adults we may have forgotten how to puzzle and marvel about why and how things happen, but young children are intently curious, and the natural world, with all its changes and transformations, attracts children's interest and invites their curiosity.

First-hand experiences

Nature can offer rich first-hand experiences that are the 'stuff' of children's learning. Rich *et al* (2005) make a powerful case for first-hand experience, which they argue are about handling and using authentic things, going to real places and meeting people, and 'being out and about in all weathers running in the wind, splashing in the rain, looking at the stars, listening to the owls, crunching through frosty leaves, jumping on the shadows, building a bonfire, collecting' (2005: 18).

Figure 2.5a Otis' drawing of the bird table with a bag of nuts as seen from the outside and from the inside.

Physical transformations

Changes in the natural world create new and exciting play materials, such as snow and ice, leaves and sticks, shadows and reflections, puddles and mud. Materials transform in seemingly magical ways, such as when water becomes ice, trapping air bubbles inside (Figure 2.6), or when water turns to steam as it is heated on a fire. Some transformations are permanent, such as when wood changes to charcoal in a fire, but some are reversible such as water and ice. Such transformations or what Athey terms 'functional dependencies' (Athey 1990: 70) are significant in children's learning. They involve an understanding of cause and effect and of permanence or reversibility.

Outdoors children are exposed to all aspects of the natural world, life and death. In thirty years of working with young children, I don't

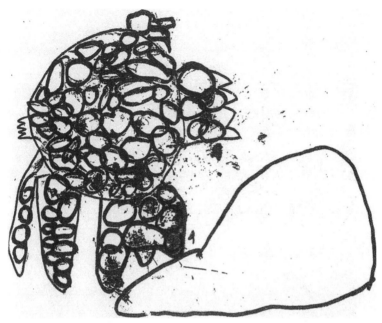

Figure 2.5b Where have all the nuts gone? The bag is empty and the bird is full.

remember any event that quite caught children's intense and focused attention as when a dead bird was found in the garden. Question followed question as children tried to understand what had happened. For example:

- Why is he dead? Why's he not moving?
- If we throw him in the air will he fly again?
- Where's his Mummy?

For many weeks after, the children played games of chase involving cats and birds illustrating how powerful first-hand experiences become the focus of attention in play. Experience of death is often screened out from young children's lives, possibly because of an understandable, but misplaced desire to protect children from upset. Yet death is as natural as life, and for children to be protected from it is to deny them the opportunity of beginning to understand the more powerfully explosive experiences of death of family or friends. Outdoors children can experience the rawness, as well as the beauty of the natural world.

Figure 2.6 Materials transform in seemingly magical ways, such as when water becomes ice, trapping air bubbles.

Constancy of nature

Although we might value a natural environment for its dynamic and ever changing characteristic, there is also a sense in which nature itself offers reassuring continuity. The laws of nature are constant and unvarying, and can provide a reassuring feeling of security that is not always present in children's more uncertain social worlds. Children quickly realize that, unlike the world of people, there is no arguing with nature. The carefully built snowman disappears on a warm day, the worm hit by a roughly handled spade will no longer offer its wriggling fascination, and water flows down hill whether you want it to or not.

Susan Isaacs made much the same point, suggesting that physical events become the test and measure of reality. 'There is no wheedling or cajoling or bullying *them*. Their answer is *yes* or *no* and remains the same to-day as yesterday' (Isaacs 1930: 80).

In a world of instant fixes, nature takes its own time and children learn how to be patient when they have to wait minutes for the snail to re-appear from its shell, hours for mud pies to harden in the sun, twenty-one days for the ducklings to hatch or weeks for the first pod to appear on their runner bean plant. Experiencing this slow pace of nature can contribute to what Benoit refers to as 'frustration tolerance' the willingness to anticipate and wait for things to happen (Benoit, cited in Jenkinson 2001).

Nature and the wider world

> True education flowers at the point when delight falls in love with responsibility. If you love something, you want to look after it.
>
> (Pullman 2005)

Although writing about a very different context, literacy, Pullman's words capture an important point. We cannot expect children to take responsibility for the natural world if they have never had a chance of experiencing it in delightful ways. Many children have more experience of nature and wildlife through electronic media than from direct first-hand experience. They are urged to protect endangered species and to save the planet, but without first experiencing the richness and beauty of the natural world for themselves. As Sobel argues:

> In our zest for making them aware of and responsible for the world's problems we cut our children off from their roots ... distancing them from rather than connecting them with the natural world.
>
> (Sobel 1996: 1–2)

It is often through play outdoors that such a relationship begins, climbing trees, making dens, rolling in leaves, watching insects, digging the ground, gardening and using nature as inspiration for imagination (Figure 2.7). When a group of children transform a bush into a

Figure 2.7 Two year olds digging for worms. First-hand experience of the natural world is essential if children are to learn to care for it.

palace, with yellow flower petals as golden treasure and sunlight as magic dust sprinkled on the floor, they are experiencing nature with powerful emotions.

Research suggests that those most committed to the natural world as campaigners or environmentalists attribute their commitment to a combination of two sources, many hours spent outdoors in a keenly-remembered wild or semi-wild place in childhood and an adult who taught respect for nature (Chawla 1990). However, there is also evidence that children and young people who have little contact with nature begin to fear it. Bixler *et al* (1994) found that many secondary school students on field trips at sixty different field centres in the USA and Canada showed fear, disgust and revulsion at natural things, seeing plants as poisonous, and insects and animals as dirty, diseased and disgusting. They showed considerably anxiety about wild spaces (who checks the woods for killers?) and some would have preferred to stay indoors. It is in the early years that children form dispositions towards the natural world, and when fears and what Sobel (1996) calls 'ecophobia' become established.

Without direct experience, it is unlikely that children will acquire a deep intuitive understanding of the natural world, which is the foundation of sustainable development. If we are to safeguard the future of life on earth, then we must allow children to develop an intimate relationship with nature, to understand, but more importantly to feel the interconnectedness of all living things and to see their own place in the world. I would argue that it is play and first-hand experience outdoors with an adult, not lessons on conservation, which forms and sustains this relationship.

Environmental campaigner Rachel Carson made a passionate plea for the place of wonder in young children's lives:

> I sincerely believe that for the child, and for the parent seeking to guide him, it is not half so important to know as to feel. If facts are the seeds that later produce knowledge and wisdom, then the emotions and the impressions of the senses are the fertile soil in which the seeds must grow. The years of early childhood are the time to prepare the soil. Once the emotions have been aroused—a sense of the beautiful, the excitement of the new and the unknown, a feeling of sympathy, pity, admiration or love—then we wish for knowledge about the object of our emotional response. Once found it has lasting meaning.
>
> (Carson 1998: 56)

> If we want children to flourish, to become truly empowered, then let us allow them to love the earth before we ask them to save it.
>
> (Sobel 1996: 39)

Movement play outdoors is vital for learning ▪

Play outdoors builds on the powerful disposition to move that is apparent from before birth. Outdoors children can engage in more exuberant play involving a wider variety of large muscle movements than indoors. They can, for example, run, jump, chase, dodge, climb, dig, slide, roll, throw, balance, swing, pedal, push and pull, all requiring different movements involving different parts of the body and different skills in co-ordinating sequences of movements. Daily bouts of moderate to vigorous physical play in early childhood, when muscles and bones are still developing, have a lasting effect on strength and endurance, as well as economy and skill of movement (Byers and Walker 1995, cited in Pellegrini and Smith 1998). Movement that raises the metabolic rate well above its resting rate is essential for long-term health and well being.

Play is a powerful motivator for vigorous movement. Games of chase and tag, pretending to be an aeroplane flying through the sky or a tiger climbing a tree provide meaning and purpose for active movement. The thrill of the chase, the joy of physical interaction, the exuberant sound effects all contribute to the enjoyment of movement as part of the play, as well as for its own sake. Children control play; they decide the pace, the place, the duration, the degree of challenge. This is very different from more formal exercise or gym classes, where children respond to adult direction, and movement is dependent on adult organization and timing. Attitudes to movement are formed early and, as in other areas of learning, it is the disposition to move that is so important, but also so vulnerable.

Movement and thought

Movement outdoors is central to young children's cognitive, as well as physical development and this can be overlooked in the concern about levels of fitness in young children. As Ouvry (2000) argues children are exercising their minds, as well as their muscles.

Piaget (cited in Athey 1990: 33) argued that 'thought is internalised action', and that young children's conceptual understanding of the world is constructed initially from movement and the sensory feedback from the child's actions on the world. Many key mathematical and scientific concepts, such as height, distance, speed, energy, space, gradient, gravity, can only really be experienced outdoors. As Athey argues, the younger the children, the more they need to experience these concepts with their whole bodies and in many different contexts. Such experiences are especially important for children with disabilities as they may be denied such opportunities in other spheres of their lives. Current research in the neurosciences appears to be confirming the importance of movement in building children's brain-minds. 'Physical exercise may boost brain function, improve mood and increase learning' (Blakemore and Frith 2005: 134).

The child sliding headfirst down a slide (Figure 2.8) is not just enjoying the exhilaration of travelling at speed down a steep slope,

Figure 2.8 Movement is vital for conceptual learning.

but is beginning to make relationships, for example, between gradient and speed. She experiences how energy is required to climb up, but not for sliding down. She uses words such as high up and low down to describe her position. Notions such as headfirst, forwards, backwards, sideways, even headfirst backwards, are examined as she varies the pattern of descent. She sees the reflections on the slide's surface and feels the coldness of the metal. Over time, she develops an awareness of friction as she sees that different fabrics of clothing or matting can impede or enhance the speed of her descent.

Movement and the importance of 'knowing your place in space'

Movement such as sliding, rolling, spinning, jumping, whirling, turning and swinging stimulate the vestibular sense, the awareness of movement in relation to the ground, which is central to balance, posture and to all spatial awareness. This awareness of our own place in space is closely linked to our emotional development, a sense of who we are. The connection between emotion and movement can be seen when a change in emotion instantly changes posture, gesture, speed and fluency of movement.

Play on the ground such as belly crawling, sliding, rolling, back pedalling and movements such as crawling, pushing and pulling, stretching and hanging, stimulate the proprioceptive sense or awareness of the body parts in relation to one another and central to the 'felt sense of self' (Greenland 2006). Such movements are central to learning (Figure 2.9). Goddard Blythe (2004) argues that an underdeveloped vestibular system can lead to clumsiness and attention problems, and contribute to later learning difficulties, for example, in reading, writing, telling the time, riding a bike and so on, all of which require awareness of balance, space and direction.

She argues that, if we attempt to feed the brain (through cognitive education), or the body alone, we do not create a 'well balanced' child (Goddard Blythe 2004: 176). Movement play outdoors can provide the nourishment the brain and body needs and at the same time provide rich 'food for thought'.

All areas of learning can be experienced outdoors

Observing insects under logs, seeing how long the ice takes to melt, hiding in an upturned box, watering the garden with a hose, listening to the sound of wind chimes, digging for ancient treasure, writing

Figure 2.9 Movement play such as swinging, twisting and turning stimulates the vestibular sense and helps develop knowledge of 'one's place in space'.

tickets for the pretend train, acting out a well loved story, smelling the newly-opened lilac are just some examples of children's play outdoors. However, they are also key experiences of scientific, mathematical, creative, historical, geographical, technological and literacy learning. Over-emphasizing the outdoors as an area for physical development, important though that is, under-emphasizes the importance of children's learning in all areas of development.

Further details about how play outdoors can offer opportunities for learning in all areas of the curriculum can be found in Edgington (2003), Bilton (2004, 2006), Callaway (2005), Ouvry (2000) and Ryder Richardson (2006).

Outdoors children can experience the curriculum in a way that makes sense to them in a context that is meaningful. Children operate at their highest level when learning makes 'human sense' to them (Donaldson 1978). Outdoors, with its emphasis on active learning, engaging first-hand experiences and challenging play opportunities provides a rich context for such meaningful learning.

Many children access these areas of learning more easily outdoors. Research suggests that boys have longer concentration spans when they are engaged in outdoor, rather than indoor activities (Hutt *et al* 1989; Dixon and Day 2004). Some boys, for example, readily take part in large scale drawing outdoors or writing in the context of play, when they may be reluctant to do so sitting at a table indoors, which can be perceived as an area for girls, or will readily build and play in dens when they might be reluctant to play in indoor home corners (Figures 2.10 and 2.11). Concern about boys' under achievement in later schooling has focused greater attention on the early dispositions to learning, and the influence of a predominantly female work force on children's play choices and access to the curriculum. Holland (2003) cautions against too simplistic a view of gender differences and urges practitioners to look more closely at their responses to the more

Figure 2.10 All areas of the curriculum can be experienced outdoors. These children are writing and measuring as part of office play.

Figure 2.11 Children may readily take part in large scale drawing outdoors.

boisterous, active, noisy play of some boys and to engage with the underlying themes of the play, rather than seeking to redirect it into more sedentary activities traditionally favoured by girls. Identifying the curriculum potential of play outdoors ensures that all children can gain access to the curriculum when they play outdoors.

Why outdoor play? A summary

Overall, there is compelling evidence for the value of outdoor play in young children's lives and learning. As we saw in Chapter 1 many children are denied access to challenging outdoor play, and this is having significant impact on their health and well being and opportunities for learning.

In summary, outdoors offers children unique opportunities, which are not available indoors. In particular, it offers young children:

- space and freedom to try things out;
- an environment that can be acted on, changed and transformed;
- a dynamic, ever-changing environment that invites exploration, curiosity and wonder;
- whole body, multi-sensory experience;
- scope to combine materials in ways that are challenging and problematic;

- opportunity to make connections in their learning;
- a rich context for curiosity, wonder, mystery and 'what if' thinking;
- space to navigate and negotiate the social world of people, friendships, to experience disagreement and resolve conflicts with peers;
- opportunity for giddy, gleeful, dizzy play;
- potential for mastery, a willingness to take risks and the skills to be safe;
- a wide range of movement opportunities that are central to learning;
- experience of the natural world and understanding of their own place within it;
- opportunities for learning in all areas of the curriculum. Some learning can only happen outdoors.

Outdoor play is about potential, and words such as 'opportunity' and 'scope for' are important here. Few of these benefits can be realized in open, windswept, asphalt surfaced playgrounds.

3

OUTDOOR PLAY: THE PRESENCE OF THE PAST

The past is not a series of mistakes which has yielded a modern enlightenment ... A feeling for the presence of the past in the present can help us contribute, with all due humility, to the future.

(Golby 1988: 58)

Provision for outdoor play is a distinctive feature of an early childhood tradition spanning over two centuries. If we are to understand the present context then it is also important that we understand the past. Yet the past is not merely a background to our work, which we occasionally look to for inspiration or to validate current practice. It is not, as Golby indicates in the quote above, just a series of mistakes from which we have moved on, nor does it represent a golden era of good practice to which we seek to return. The past is, instead, an inescapable part of the present. Ideas and practices are not invented by each new generation, but evolve, losing some bits here, gaining new emphasis there, some parts remaining buried to be re-discovered later with new impetus and meaning.

Traditions are not fixed and resistant to change, but are dynamic and evolving, and it is important that we capture that 'presence of the past', but reinterpret it in helping to shape the future. It is not sufficient to justify an area of provision such as outdoor play by reference to the pioneers working in very different contexts. Rather, we need to look more critically at their ideas and reinterpret them in a contemporary context.

In this chapter, I look at just four distinctive pioneers who have shaped our understanding of outdoor play: Friedrich Froebel, Maria Montessori, Margaret McMillan, Susan Isaacs and Marjorie Allen, better known as Lady Allen of Hurtwood. What were their perspectives on outdoor play and on risk and challenge?

Friedrich Froebel (1782–1852)

To Froebel, the garden was both literal and metaphorical. He used the word kindergarten, a garden for children, rather than the word school and saw the kindergarten as a place where the child could develop in harmony with nature. Educators would provide a rich environment for growth, and would tend, nurture and cultivate each child just as a good gardener would tend a young plant. Froebel believed in a divine unity and connectedness between all living things, and it was therefore important for children to be close to nature in the outdoor environment.

The garden was an essential part of the kindergarten he created in Blankenburg, Germany and represented the essence of Froebel's holistic philosophy where learning was not compartmentalized, but everything was linked. The garden included open spaces for the children's play, and for the specially devised action songs, ring games and music. There was a paved area with seats for parents and visitors. The central area consisted of single plots of ground for each child, or if there was not enough space, for two children to share as 'connections of twos in the kindergarten has something good in it, it teaches friendliness and each child is so much the richer for what the other puts in the bed' (Froebel, cited in Herrington 1998: 330). These individual beds were surrounded by a path and by communal plots for flowers, fruit and vegetables. Froebel even specified the dimensions of the path to ensure that it was wide enough for two children to pass along together. Children could arrange and grow what they liked in their own plots, but they had to work together in the communal gardens and take responsibility for them.

Significantly, all of Froebel's garden designs showed the individual plots surrounded by the communal gardens. 'The part for the general is the enclosing, as it were the protecting part; that for the children the enclosed, protected part' (Froebel, cited in Herrington 2001). This was no mere arrangement; rather it illustrated, in a tangible form, Froebel's philosophy of unity in all things, and the connectedness between individual and community, freedom and responsibility, work and play. The individual was protected, even embraced by the community, but also had a responsibility to it.

Through gardening and play outdoors children learnt about nature and about the growth of plants and animals, but they also learnt to care for and take responsibility for nature, and gradually to recognize their own place in the natural world. It was not a place for didactic lessons in nature study or for teaching skills of horticulture. Rather, children learnt through activity and experience. The garden then was educative, but only through children's own activity. Children learnt through first-hand experience and 'not the mere explanations of words and ideas which are of no interest' (Froebel, cited in Herrington 2001: 311).

Provision was responsive to close observation of children's play and use of materials. For example, Froebel observed how much children enjoyed trying to use the adult-sized wheelbarrow in the garden so he arranged for forty small wheelbarrows to be made for the children to use independently. Children were encouraged to take responsibility for the wider environment of the local community and 'the sight of Froebel leading his cheerful group of children through the town and each pushing a wheelbarrow and picking up litter wherever they went, must have amused and amazed the citizens of Blankenburg' (Leibschner 1992: 26).

Children's freely chosen games outdoors were a source of fascination to Froebel. He saw in such games evidence of children's growing sense of justice, self-control, comradeship and fairness. He acknowledged that there was many a rough word or act, but also evidence of tolerance and care of those who were weaker, younger or new to the game. Such games had a 'mighty power to awaken and to strengthen the intelligence and the soul as well as the body'. He therefore argued that, in addition to the kindergarten, every town should have a playground where children could meet and play (Liebschner 1992: 52).

Space for children extended beyond the garden and Froebel included regular excursions to the surrounding landscapes and it is interesting to note that Froebel's very first recorded lesson took place outdoors in the village stream, where teacher and children dammed the flow of water to work out the effect of erosion (Liebschner 1992):

> Show him his valley in its whole; . . . he should follow his brook or rivulet from its source to its mouth; . . . he should also explore the elevated ridges, so that he may see the ranges and spurs of mountains; he should climb the highest summits, so that he may know the entire region in its unity . . . This direct and indirect observation of things themselves, and their actual living connections in nature, and not the mere explanation of words and ideas which are of no interest to a boy, should waken in him, vaguely at first but ever more clearly the great thought of inner, constant living unity of all things and phenomena in nature.
>
> (Froebel, cited in Herrington 1998: 32)

Froebel observed children's play outdoors and identified the educational potential of natural materials. For example, children could learn about cause and effect and physical processes as they played with water outdoors:

> He makes a little garden by his father's fence, maps out a river's course in the cart track or ditch, studies the effects of the fall and pressure on his small water wheel, or observes a piece of flat wood or bark as it floats on the water which he had dammed to form a pool.
>
> (Lilley 1967: 127)

Froebel's garden then was a spiritual place where children could grow and develop in harmony with nature, and begin to sense their own place in the natural world. It was a place for creative and imaginative play for investigation and discovery for songs, music and ring games. Froebel was perhaps unique amongst the pioneers in linking garden design to his philosophy of children's learning and in recognizing the holistic nature of young children's learning. The garden was a place where parents, teachers and children could play and work together.

Maria Montessori (1869–1952)

For Montessori, working in a poor inner city community in Rome, Italy it was not the garden, but the 'house' that was the enduring metaphor for her approach to early childhood. The environment, she argued, should allow children to be like masters in their own houses, that is it should be child-sized, offer independent movement and be well organized with everything in its place. It was not nature, but science and her notion of 'scientific pedagogy', which was a guiding principle. Using Froebel's metaphor of the gardener she argued that 'behind the good cultivator . . . stands the scientist'. Scientific knowledge helps not only to a better knowledge of the plants, 'but can be used to transform them'. She gives examples of the double carnations and giant thornless roses as the 'supra nature', which can be achieved with the help of science (Montessori 1989: 9). This is a very different philosophy from Froebel's garden where weeds were valued as much as the flowers.

Montessori's first 'Children's House' was amongst the slums of inner city Rome. The garden was within a central courtyard surrounded by tenement flats and the space consisted of open areas for running and playing games with hoops, balls and ropes, as well as a garden bordered with trees for shade. The gardens were for cultivating plants and vegetables and like Froebel's garden included individual plots for each child. There was, she argued, nothing new in the idea of a garden for children:

> The novelty lies perhaps in my idea for the use of this space, which is to be in direct communication with the schoolroom so that children may be free to go and come as they like, throughout the entire day.
>
> (Montessori 1920: 81)

It was Montessori, therefore, who pioneered the idea of open access from indoors to outdoors and free choice and self-direction, but 'choice' was restricted. The outdoor space was not a space for the imagination nor was it a space for play. 'If I were persuaded that children needed to play I would have provided the proper apparatus, but I am not so persuaded' (Montessori, cited in Bruce 1984: 80). Children could carry out their mats and work on structured apparatus outdoors, but the apparatus was to be used only in one way and could not be transformed imaginatively as symbols, she argued, detracted from the real world.

Unlike Froebel, Montessori did not believe that natural materials were educative and, therefore, she made no provision for play materials like sand and water. Rather, she argued that structured materials, which had been 'subject to the perfecting hand of a higher intelligence' (Montessori 1983: 47), were necessary to identify the 'real' or 'true' nature of the child. She claimed, through her didactic apparatus and her conditions of freedom, to have discovered the normal child, a natural child, a uniformity of type, a 'model child'. All behaviour problems she argued disappeared, but so also did 'creative imagination, delight in stories, attachment to persons, . . . play, . . . imitation, curiosity, all disappeared and there remains only one kind of child, the normalised child' (Montessori 1949: 162). There was, therefore, a particular tension between Montessori's idea of freedom and the restrictions she placed on what Froebel argued were characteristics of children and, indeed, of humanity, but it is a reminder that freedom is a porous term, it takes on the values of those who use it. It is freedom to 'do what' that matters.

Children were encouraged to water the plants, and to feed and care for the chickens, but such activities were essentially to develop physical dexterity, for example, in opening and closing the latch to the chicken coop, independence and moral responsibility, rather than fostering curiosity or developing knowledge of plants and animals.

Clearly, Froebel and Montessori offered very different approaches to the garden. Froebel valued games, stories and symbolic play outdoors. The symbol was of the essence, whereas Montessori believed that symbols encouraged illusion and diverted children's attention from the real world. Froebel emphasized the creatively active and curious child who could explore the natural environment, including materials such as sand and water, experiment with them and transform them. Learning, Montessori believed, moved from parts to the whole, whereas to Froebel the whole context must be experienced first. While Froebel emphasized Nature, Montessori emphasized Science. Froebel valued play and work with adults, while Montessori valued independent and concentrated work. Yet while Froebel was rather ambivalent about the degree of direction required Montessori pioneered the idea of free choice and free movement indoors and out.

Margaret McMillan (1860–1931)

Margaret McMillan was a socialist politician, a social reformer and campaigner working in England at the end of the nineteenth and beginning of the twentieth century. Her experience of running an open air camp for children in the slums of Deptford, South London, where disease was rife, convinced her that time spent outdoors could dramatically improve children's health and that the youngest children should be the focus of attention. She developed an open air nursery school for children, and literally designed and built a garden for children. The garden was central and the indoor spaces were merely shelters for use in very bad weather. Everything, she argued, could take place outdoors, play, sleep, meals, stories, and games:

> The garden is the essential matter. Not the lesson or the pictures or the talk. The lessons and talk are about things seen and done in the garden, just as the best of all the paintings in the picture galleries are shadows of originals now available to children of the open air.
>
> (McMillan 1930: 2)

McMillan was a Froebelian and claimed to have nothing to do with Montessori, although she was influenced, as was Montessori, by the didactic 'sense training' of Seguin. She argued that there was no need for artificial didactic apparatus to stimulate children's senses in isolation when real first-hand experience offered richer and more meaningful opportunities:

> Suppose you want to develop the touch sense! Lo! Here are a score of leaves, hairy sunflower, crinkled primrose, glossy fuschia, and the rose. Do you want to compare colours, to note

hues and shades? Well here is wealth a plenty. The herb garden will offer more scents than anyone can put into a box, and a very little thought will make of every pathway a riot of opportunities.

(McMillan, cited in Bradburn 1989: 17)

As Bruce points out, 'the riot of opportunities and the real flowers rather than apparatus is more Froebelian in influence, whilst the "you want to develop the touch sense" is influenced by the programmed approach of Seguin' (Bruce 1991: 47). Advice to adults to ask such questions as 'What is the biggest leaf in the garden? What colour is it? Show me the blue flowers' reflects the influence of Montessori's didactic approach. The two perspectives do not sit easily together and this tension is evident in her underpinning approach to the garden.

McMillan literally designed and built her garden for children, clearing and transforming a derelict site into a landscaped garden. The garden was arranged on different levels, on grass and hard surfaces. There were paths, steps and open spaces, logs, climbing bars, slides, banks, ropes, swings, shrubberies, sheds and playhouses. Everything was designed and provided for some reason. Steps, for example, were not just functional, but provided important places for jumping on and off, and provided valuable practice for 'little people who are learning to go up and down' (McMillan 1919: 49).

There was a horticulture section consisting of a herb garden, kitchen garden, rock garden, and wild garden. 'Children love a wilderness. So one plot should be allowed to grow wild but many beautiful things can be planted in it' (McMillan 1919: 47). The vegetables, fruits and herbs were harvested, and used in the nursery kitchens in order to improve the children's diet. Significantly, the children helped the gardener grow the produce, rather than take responsibility for their own plot as in Froebel's garden. However, they did have their own patch of ground for digging and exploring. All the plants and flowers were chosen for their sensory qualities of colour, patterns, scent, texture and, where appropriate, taste.

There were areas for climbing with bars and planks for sliding. Ropes and more importantly trees were considered 'the finest kind of apparatus for climbing you can ever have' (McMillan 1919: 23). Other areas provided opportunity for building, and for imaginative play with boxes, wheels, ladders, planks, barrels and ropes. A wide range of animals and birds were included in the garden including rabbits, guinea-pigs, ponds with aquatic life and chickens. The dove cote, perhaps inspired by Froebel's activity song of the same name, housed breeding doves.

As well as the wild garden, McMillan included a junk heap:

Every child needs a bigger world than the one we are getting ready for him. Our green plots and ordered walks are good and right but who does not remember that he once liked to play in a big place where there were no walks at all and no rules?

Therefore a nursery garden must have a free and rich place, a great rubbish heap, stones, and flints, bits of can, and old iron and pots. Here every healthy child will want to go, taking out things of his own choosing to build with.

(McMillan 1919: 47)

Such a junk heap was, she noted, the most popular after the making of mud hills and trenches, and the filling of dams and rivers (McMillan 1930: 76).

Inevitably, McMillan's garden changed over time. It could be argued that it became more structured with more fixed apparatus, such as slides, and climbing frames and less 'simple and improvised' (McMillan 1919: 46). The 1930 edition of her book *The Nursery School*, published a year before she died, placed less emphasis on the junk heap, the tool shed and the jumping off steps, suggesting that these were no longer considered appropriate in the 1930s.

McMillan recognized the supreme importance of health and well-being for children's development and learning. The garden was surrounded by tenement flats and central to the community so that people could watch and learn about children's play. It offered diversity and rich sensory experience. Straw (1990) argued that McMillan's vision for the garden declined not because it was found wanting, but because its purpose and value was misunderstood. The garden came to be perceived narrowly as a place to promote good health for disadvantaged children—a compensatory model—rather than a play and learning environment for all children.

Susan Isaacs (1885–1948)

Susan Isaacs worked in a very different social context from McMillan. She opened the Malting House School in Cambridge in 1924, a school for highly advantaged children of professional parents. It was an experimental school that had two central aims: 'to stimulate the active enquiry of the children themselves rather than to teach them' and 'to bring within their immediate experience every range of fact to which their interests reached out' (Isaacs 1930: 17). Children were given considerable freedom for Isaacs argued that 'play has the greatest value for the child when it is really free and his own' (Isaacs 1929: 133).

The garden included grass, fruit trees, a climbing frame, slides, movable ladders, trees for climbing, flower and vegetable gardens with individual plots for each child and a range of animals, including chickens, guinea-pigs, as well as snakes and salamanders.

A journalist from the *Spectator*, making a film about the school, provides a colourful description of the Malting House Garden:

> For a short half hour I watched children of from four to nine years of age having the time of their lives, wading up to their knees trying to fix a sandpit with water, mending a tap with a spanner, oiling the work of a clock, joyously feeding a bonfire, dissecting crabs, climbing on scaffolding, weighing each other on a seesaw, in fact doing all those things which every child delights in doing.
>
> (cited in Van der Eyken 1975: 56)

The garden provoked children's curiosity and enquiry. It offered challenge and risk and children had considerable freedom to try things out, to question, to experiment and to follow wherever their curiosity led. However, this freedom also had constraints. For example, children were allowed to build and light fires, but only one box of matches was given to each child and fires were not to be built near to the wooden summer house. Children were allowed to climb on the summer house roof, but only one child was allowed at a time. As Drummond (2000: 3) points out this was a much more daring and child friendly rule that contains within it an implicit invitation to climb! Children could use a range of gardening and woodwork tools like saws and hammers, but these were not to be used in a threatening manner and must always be returned after use. Like Froebel and Montessori before her she argued that freedom brought responsibility, but it also empowered children to develop the skills to be safe:

> The children climbed trees and ladders, used tools and handled fire and matches far more freely than is commonly allowed, and with complete immunity—partly no doubt, because of our careful supervision but largely also because their skill and poise became so good under these conditions.
>
> (Isaacs 1930: 25)

Isaacs' view of childhood was one of passion. Young children had a passion for finding out about and striving to understand the world. 'The thirst for understanding ... springs from the child's deepest emotional needs ... [it is] a veritable passion' (Isaacs 1932: 113). Isaacs was not only an educator and a scientist, she had also trained with Melanie Klein and was a practising psychoanalyst. Play, there-fore, was seen as an outlet for strong impulses and for expression of strong emotion.

There was nothing soft or romantic about Isaacs' view of children and play. She noted children's raw, angry and sometimes destructive behaviour, as well as their extreme gentleness and tenderness. The garden was a place of enormous fascination and source of learning about the world, but it was also a safe place to vent their frustrations and anger. At the same time they developed awareness of others and responsibility for other living things. She noted when children's curi-osity led them to pull worms in half and she allowed them to dig up the dead pet rabbit when they were curious as to what had happened to it, but she firmly stopped them from harming a spider or stamping on insects. She acknowledged children's curiosity about death and with the detached approach of a scientist, she regularly dissected dead animals with the children so that they could see and learn about the inner organs.

Although she tried to observe children in free conditions she also recognized, unlike Montessori, that it was impossible to discover the 'natural child':

> Rather we have come to realise that most of the behaviour of children . . . in these years will be highly complex in its sources and springs. It will for instance always have some reference, implicit or explicit, to what adults expect—or to what children imagine that adults expect.
>
> (Isaacs 1930: 8)

Malting House School was open for only four years, but its legacy has been long lasting. Isaacs' meticulous documentation of children's behaviour, thinking and emotions are still as vibrant and fascinating today.

Marjorie Allen (Lady Allen of Hurtwood) 1897–1976

Lady Allen is featured less in education literature, but nevertheless deserves an important place as a pioneer of outdoor play areas for young children. Lady Allen was an architect, author, socialist, pacifist and prolific campaigner for the rights of children. She had a signifi-cant impact on policy and practice for children in England in the mid-twentieth century. Although not an educator she was active in campaigning for better provision for young children and became president of the Nursery School Association, and a founder member of the world wide Organization Mondiale pour L'Education Prescolaire (OMEP). Lady Allen designed play areas for many nursery schools, including gardens with sand pits and paddling pools on roof tops of blocks of flats in Camden, London.

However, she is associated most for bringing the idea of adventure or junk playgrounds to Britain. Junk playgrounds originated in Denmark in the 1940s. A Danish architect and landscape designer observed that children were much more interested in playing on building sites after work was finished at the end of the day than in specially constructed playgrounds. The first junk playground opened in Copenhagen under the leadership of John Bertelson, a Froebel trained teacher. At that time, Denmark was under German occupation and 'the playground was hidden from view by a six-foot bank topped with a fence as if children's play represented something of a rebellion to occupation and needed to be hidden' (Norman 2003: 17).

Marjorie Allen visited the Copenhagen playground in 1946 and was impressed with the wealth of play opportunities that waste materials provided and the lack of fixed and made equipment. Children improvised their own play spaces constructing them from discarded timber, and a variety of tools and nails. They could experiment with sand, water, fire under the eye of a trained play leader. Through her writing and campaigning she was influential in the growth of a grass roots movement of adventure playgrounds in major cities in the UK, particularly in London where bomb sites and waste ground could be transformed into spaces for children. She argued that:

> Children seek access to a place where they can dig in the earth, build huts and dens with timber, use real tools, experiment with fire and water, take really great risks and learn to overcome them. They want a place where they can create and destroy, where they can build their own worlds, with their own skills at their own time and in their own way. In our built up towns, they never find these opportunities. They're frustrated at every turn or tidied out of existence.
>
> (Allen, cited in Rich *et al* 2005: 46)

Using the term 'adventure', rather than junk playground she campaigned for 'do it yourself' play environments where all children especially children with disabilities who were marginalized from conventional playgrounds, could engage in creative and imaginative play. Her famously provocative statement 'better a broken bone than a broken spirit' sums up her belief in the importance of exciting, challenging and adventurous play and the damage that can be caused if such experience is denied to children:

> Small children ... need a place where they can develop self–
> reliance, where they can test their limbs, their senses and their
> brain, so that brain, limbs and senses gradually become obedient
> to their will. If, during these early years, a child is deprived of
> the opportunity to educate himself by trial and error, by taking
> risks and by making friends, he may, in the end, lose confidence
> in himself and lose his desire to become self reliant. Instead of
> learning security he becomes fearful and withdrawn.
>
> (Allen 1968: 14)

She was damning in her criticism of conventional playgrounds that
are static, dull, unchallenging, and which do not account for young
children's drive to explore, imagine, create and to seek companionship. The tendency for 'ordering a complete playground from a catalogue is greatly to be deplored: this lack of enterprise spells dullness
and monotony and only the manufacturers benefit' (Allen 1968: 140).
'Why are so many of the new playgrounds stagnant? And why are so
many expensive mistakes made over and over again?' (Allen 1968: 15).
Why indeed? The question is as relevant today as it was in the 1960s.

Many adventure playgrounds closed after the 1974 Health and
Safety at Work Act as Local Authorities were unwilling to risk litigation
over such potentially risky environments (Chilton, 2003). Nevertheless, Lady Allen's vision for challenging outdoor play environments,
her belief that children with disabilities were entitled to equally rich
and exciting environments, and her knowledge, from careful observation, of the impact of design on children's play is still influential
today particularly in the playwork field.

What is the essence of this tradition?

We have inherited a rich tradition of outdoor play and the nursery
garden and evidence of this diverse tradition can be seen in practice
today. It is tempting to pick and mix different parts of the tradition,
but such an eclectic approach is not a strong basis for moving forward
because, ultimately, we have to make choices based on our own
values and vision for children, as well as research evidence.

While there are very real differences between these pioneers, there
are also some commonalities. All, in different ways emphasized:

- the educative potential of the garden and the outdoor environment
  beyond;
- the value of time spent outdoors, and the importance of contact
  with nature and gardening;

- respect for children and trust in their competence to do things for themselves;
- risk taking and adventurousness;
- children learning through active engagement and first-hand experience;
- design of space that is underpinned by theoretical principles and close observation of children;
- involving parents and the wider community in children's learning outdoors.

All but Montessori placed a strong emphasis on the creative and imaginative child, and saw free play and talk as powerful vehicles for learning. Froebel was perhaps unique in translating his philosophy of education into a garden design, and in recognizing how such design was connected to children's play and behaviour. He also saw the design of the garden as a landscape for children's learning, which was connected to the wider landscape of the child's life. Froebel's philosophy reconciled what were seemingly opposites, play and work, imagination and reality, freedom and control, individuality and community.

What has happened to this rich heritage?

It is not difficult to find settings where outdoor provision bears no relation at all to what it originally was. Gone is the nursery garden, and in its place is a patch of tarmac or soft spongy surface, an assorted collection of low level plastic equipment offering little challenge, some tired relics of neglected plants, numerous bikes in various states of repair, adults looking at their watches wondering when their 'shift' outdoors will end. This may be a dismal picture, but it is certainly not untypical. What do these outdoor environments say about our priorities for young children in contemporary society?

However, there are also play areas and early childhood settings that catch some of the visionary qualities of the pioneers, offering exciting and dynamic environments underpinned by a clear rationale one, which is continually reflected on and reappraised.

Re-examining the principles of the pioneers forces us to reflect critically on our own view of childhood, and our own approach to the purpose and value of the outdoor play space. What sort of environment do we want for children? Is it a place of passionate enquiry, a place of adventure where fantasy and imagination thrive? Can children access all areas of learning outdoors? What are the freedoms that we want for children and what constraints will best allow those freedoms to thrive? Can children move freely between indoors and outdoors? What will we add to the tradition to pass on to other generations?

As the centre of learning has in many cases shifted from the outdoors to the indoors, resulting in practices that are pale imitations of what they originally were, we urgently need a critical reappraisal of the purpose and value of the outdoor area, which is willing to engage with visions from the past to help shape a more dynamic and exciting future.

> Tradition is seen as an ongoing process which does not die out but whose manifestations in forms, beliefs and activities wax and wane and transform, making perceivable lineage and setting in motion new ones through time and across geographical space.
>
> (Bishop and Curtis 2001: 10)

These words refer to another important tradition, that of children's evolving playground culture, but are just as relevant to our thinking about the nursery garden tradition. The onus is on us to play with our inheritance, ensure that it is vibrant, open to new influences, continually reappraised, but not to throw it away, squander it or bury it under a layer of tarmac or rubberized safety surface.

4

SPACES AND PLACES FOR PLAY

The Universe is revealed to me not as a space, imposing a massive presence to which I can only adapt, but as a scope, a domain which takes shape as I act upon it.

(Paulo Freire 1972: 65)

Where do we start when designing or re-designing outdoor play spaces? Frequently the process starts with play providers leafing through equipment catalogues with a 'lets have one of those' attitude. However, this is starting in the wrong place. The starting place has to be what we want for children and what they want for play. We need to ask ourselves questions like:

- What do we want this place to look and feel like?
- What makes a good space for children and why?
- What values about children and learning underpin it?

Designing outdoor spaces for children

There are three fundamental points that underpin the approach taken in this chapter.

First, an outdoor environment is never neutral, rather it reflects values about children, their learning and development. It communicates powerful messages about what is deemed important or trivial. As Titman (1994) has argued, children 'read' their environment as a set of symbols indicating what they are expected to do, think and feel in that place. An open space full of climbing equipment and bikes communicates that this is a place for physical exercise. An area where the surface space is covered by number lines, alphabet stepping stones, shapes of different colours suggests that this is a place where learning about colours, shapes and letters matters more than play. A space covered in rubber safety matting and filled with bright coloured plastic toys communicates that children need to be protected from the real world of rich sensory experiences.

Underpinning the approach taken in this chapter and, indeed, the whole book is a view of young children as curious, enquiring, puzzling, as playful, creative and imaginative, as competent and capable and closely engaged with other children and adults, and with the natural world. Design of space should be underpinned by the evidence that young children learn best through rich first-hand experience, play and talk and thrive best when they are emotionally secure, joyful and in close relationships with others. Clearly, this view of children requires, indeed demands, a very different environment from the examples given previously.

Secondly, children do not just see the outdoor environment as spaces full of 'things', but also as places full of meaning. Gibson's theory of 'affordance' is useful here as he argues that our perceptual experiences include not only things and events in the environment, but more fundamentally their functional meaning (Gibson, in Heft 1988: 29). Environmental features 'afford' or offer certain possibilities so that 'things' are much more than their physical characteristics, but instead become, for example, climb-on-able, climb over-able, crawl under-able. So, depending on their age, children might see a fallen tree trunk as affording scope for pulling up to stand, sitting, straddling, galloping, balancing, or even pushing and rolling. Its texture might invite patting or stroking, prodding or crumbling and the living creatures housed within it provoke curiosity and investigation. Its shape offers potential for imaginative transformation with features of the tree such as crevices, bumps, patterns taking on a whole new meaning in play. From this perspective, features of the environment 'afford' multi-dimensional play possibilities, which are not always recognized by adults.

Thirdly, an outdoor environment for young children is a dynamic living place constantly changing as children and adults transform it. It is not a static predetermined layout to which children have to adapt, nor is it just a scenic backdrop for a series of 'activities', rather it is a domain that takes shape as children or children and adults inhabit it. Children interact with the environment almost like a play partner, shaping and transforming it, but in turn being shaped by the experiences and interactions it enables. It should not be a space for children to play 'in' with equipment for children to play 'on' (Herrington 1997). Rather, it is a series of spaces for children to explore and experiment,

Figure 4.1 A dead tree trunk affords many opportunities for play. These children are filling the hollow trunk with ceanothus flowers from a nearby bush. First they make poison then magic medicine. A complex narrative unfolds.

create and imagine, engage with others and create their own meaningful places. Children, then, should be 'authors', as well as 'readers' of their environments.

Listening to children

Design of space must take account of children's ideas and perspectives. Listening to children is much more than just a consultation exercise. It involves a view of children as experts in their own lives that is deeply respectful of children as thinkers and learners with ideas that are worth listening to. It acknowledges that children create meaning out of space and that these meanings may be very different from our own.

This approach is very different from 'consultation', which can be fraught with problems and simply asking children what they would like in their play area can lead to 'more of the same' as children request what they already know. At worst it is used as a way of validating what has already been decided.

The Mosaic approach (Clark and Moss 2005, 2006) influenced by the Reggio Emilia 'pedagogy of listening' offers more innovative ways of gathering young children's perspectives through, for example, children's own photographs, maps, books and tours of the environment. The approach provides a tool for identifying the multiple meanings that individuals and groups of children attach to their environment. For example, three-year-old Gary identified his favourite place outdoors as 'the cave' where he spent time 'listening to magic music from my magic radio' (Clark, 2005: 1). The researcher was surprised to find that the 'cave' was not a dark corner of the play area as expected, but a curved bench on the grass. She had identified the bench as a social place, but to Gary it was a private world of his own imagination. Clearly, listening to and observing children can challenge our preconceived ideas and assumptions about spaces for play. It requires a willingness to be open to others' views and the meanings that they make, to be prepared to suspend our own judgements and to challenge our assumptions.

Design of children's space then involves listening to children, trying to see the world through children's eyes. However, it also means interpreting their ideas using our knowledge about children's play and learning, and available research on children's use of space. It should be a collaborative venture with educators, landscape architects, gardeners, children, parents and the local community engaged in a dialogue about what makes an effective space for play and learning.

Why spaces and places?

We often think of space as being empty or 'nothing', but space is defined by its surroundings. It has surfaces, contours and boundaries. Space has dimensions of size and shape; it has qualities of openness or enclosure. It can be vast and infinite, or closed and intimate. Shape enables certain movements and behaviours, and inhibits others. Its sensory qualities can influence mood, we feel and behave differently in an open windswept space compared with a sheltered enclosed space.

Place is much more than space. Place is space imbued with feelings and meaning. While space can be anonymous, place has significance and meaning in our lives. We feel attachments to a place and such attachments would appear to be an important human need and a way in which we gain a sense of self and belonging in the world. Tuan, a geographer who has researched notions of space and place, argues that place is less abstract than space:

> What begins as undifferentiated space becomes place as we get to know it better and endow it with value . . . The ideas 'space' and 'place' require each for definition. From the security and stability of place we are aware of the openness, freedom and threat of space and vice versa.
>
> (Tuan 1977: 6)

Young children transform space for their own purposes. They endow space with meaning and, as we have seen, these meanings can be very different from our own.

Incidental features for play

Children do not experience outdoor environments as just physical spaces, but as places with meaning. They make their own meaning from seemingly insignificant features of the physical environment— those which to adults appear to have no apparent function at all. For example, an odd shaped corner of the play area becomes the best place to cover your eyes in a game of hide and seek; a mundane drain is used for a game of posting stones; the crumbling mortar in an old brick wall is transformed into gun powder in a game of war or at other times as 'sugar' to sprinkle on sand cakes. Brian Little refers to these as 'Sweet Nothings . . . the pleasant, casual, seemingly inconsequential exchanges between children and their environment that give quiet delight' (Little, cited in Titman 1994: 12).

I remember as a child how an old metal railing became the focus of endless games not only for swinging and somersaulting, but also for imagining and communicating. The hollow metal tubes included a few well-spaced holes, which were used as telephones and because the sound was magnified we could communicate with friends over some distance. The holes in the railings also became secret places where we posted messages to each other, such as carefully folded scraps of paper, or tiny gifts, such as a farthing wrapped up in a sweet paper. I still remember, many years later, the intense disappointment on seeing the railings replaced by shiny new ones, without the hollow spaces, which had provided hours of rich and satisfying play.

Research has confirmed this tendency for children to make meaning from seemingly insignificant features of the environment (Armitage 2001; Factor 2004). Armitage, for example, although observing children in middle, rather than early childhood, identified how metal grills and fences became jails in games of cops and robbers, drain covers were the focus of elaborate marble games, holes in seats or tree trunks were used as witches' cauldrons with pebbles, grasses and small flowers added to make witches' brew. These were not just transitory episodes of play, but became part of the culture of the play area. The same features assumed similar significance years later, with an entirely new population of children illustrating how deeply rooted and long-lasting children's play culture can be when mixed age groups of children play together. Play traditions evolve over time with each new generation of children adding to and re-shaping them.

Incidental features, then, can assume great symbolic significance and it is important that adults 'read' and tune in to the culture of the play area. Where adults might see only ugliness, irrelevance or mere functionality children often see play potential. Designing outdoor play areas must take account of children's propensity to notice and make use of odd spaces, corners, fences, posts, holes, gaps, grills and drains. Incidental patterns on wall and ground surfaces, such as lines, edgings, grids, circles and zigzags are often incorporated into play. In contrast, fixed playground markings, after an initial flurry of interest, tend, in my experience, to be ignored.

As design of space becomes increasingly prepackaged, there is a danger that the odd corners, niches, nooks and crannies, which we know provide endless fascination for children's play, are eliminated. The end result can be neat and ordered play areas, but with little heart or soul, and without the very features that can contribute to a rich play culture and a strong sense of 'place'.

What makes a good space for play?

Although we know that children will adapt the most unlikely of environments into places for play; nevertheless, if we are creating outdoor spaces for play then we need to consider what features contribute to a good space for children's play and learning.

Considering the literature on environments, as well as children's learning there is evidence that design of challenging and creative outdoor environment for young children is likely to include the following spaces:

- designated and connected spaces;
- elevated spaces;
- wild spaces;
- spaces for exploring and investigating;
- spaces for mystery and enchantment;
- natural spaces;
- space for the imagination;
- spaces for movement and stillness;
- social spaces;
- fluid spaces.

These are now examined in more depth.

Designated and connected spaces

Many writers suggest that outdoor space should be subdivided into designated areas. (Bilton 2002: 48), for example, argues that the outdoors should be organized into discrete areas or zones for different sorts of play. She suggests that there should be areas for imaginative play, building and construction, gymnasium, horticulture, as well as a science area and a quiet area. Mountain (2001) also argues that there should be clearly defined areas, and these should include areas for cognitive, social, physical and imaginative play.

While there might be some benefit in using these categories to think about or reflect on existing provision, the danger is that our thinking becomes constrained by the boundaries of the categories and our attention is focused on the space within such demarcations, rather than the links and connections between them. Too rigid an interpretation of zones can result in areas that are inflexible, predictable and stereotyped.

Given that all aspects of children's learning and development are interrelated then it is important that design of space should both reflect and support this. A 'gymnasium' area, for example, can focus adults' and children's attention on the physical aspects of development, but possibly at the expense of the social, the imaginative or the cognitive dimensions. Clearly, physical, social and imaginative activity is integral to cognitive learning and cannot realistically be separated.

Children do not necessarily use spaces according to the preconceived purposes of the adults who plan them. Rather they are 'nomads of the environment and great manipulators of space' (Vechi

1998: 131). Play areas that allow children to be 'nomadic' in their use of resources and space, to inhabit areas for their own purposes and create their own play places is more consistent with our understanding of play as flowing through space and time

This does not mean that the organization of space should be random or that play areas should end up as a cluttered mass of disconnected parts, where play is constantly interrupted or impeded by other play, or where children spend time trying to navigate the parts, rather than owning or transforming the spaces themselves. As Jilk (2005) argues too much flexibility can impede the development of a sense of 'place'. Careful planning of certain fixed areas, such as a sand area, garden area, digging area, construction area, and significant landmarks, such as a pergola, a tree where stories are told, a bridge or a mound, help children, particularly those with disabilities, to navigate the area and can contribute to a sense of 'place'.

Connected spaces

Space should enable, rather than inhibit the fluid nature of play. Fluid, rather than solid blocks of space and clear pathways encourage links between different aspects of play provision, and between indoors and outdoors. Play features placed nearby can 'invite' children to make connections. For example, a water tap placed near the sand pit will encourage children to combine sand and water, and thereby transform it into a new material for exploring and moulding. A path leading from a sand area to a smaller sand pit some distance away will encourage toddlers to transport sand between the two areas. A speaking tube can encourage communication between different play features, and between indoors and outdoors. Pathways or stepping stones, bridges and board walks can invite play to move into new areas so that, much as on a journey, there are new pathways and territories to explore, new choices to be made, but known pathways with opportunities to return to a secure place as well. Too often pathways or vehicle roadways are fixed in circular or figure of eight formations resulting in a 'hamster cage effect' of perpetual circular motion, which can isolate other areas.

Children are social beings and often want to engage with what is going on around them. Rigid boundaries, such as solid walls and fences isolate and separate children, whereas peep holes, openings in fences, gaps in planting allow children to have some privacy, but also to connect with what is going on in other spaces. The trend towards walled or cage-like perimeter fences designed to keep children 'in' and strangers 'out' is a worrying feature of some contemporary design. Herrington (2005a,b) argues that outside fences should not cut

Figure 4.2 Children find their own ways of connecting with the space beyond.

children off, but rather should invite children to look over or through in order to see and experience the wider world.

Everyday events outside the space, such as dogs being walked, deliveries made, roads dug or street lights mended are a source of fascination for children, but also a rich source of play material. Corsaro (2003: 49) noted how children in an Italian kindergarten watched the refuse collectors' daily rounds and 'waving to the garbage man' became a daily event, which entered the culture of the play area and still featured in a new generation of children's play a year later. I recently observed children playing 'building' using a bucket on the end of a rope to lift bricks up onto the roof of a play house. The inspiration for this had come from watching the building work on a nearby roof where pulleys and ropes were used to lift the tiles. In this sense, the boundaries between the play and the non-play space, between 'inside' and 'outside' become blurred.

The more opportunities there are for children to make connections between different areas of experience, the richer the structures of thought (Athey 1990). For example, if the environment includes one fixed slide, children can experience gradient and maybe the impact of friction on speed of descent. However, if the environment includes ramps, sloping pathways, planks at varying heights, grass banks and so on, children have the opportunity to make connections between these experiences, and begin to understand the relationship between the angle and the surface material of the slope and the speed of the descent, and thereby build a richer concept of gradient.

Making a connection between seemingly unconnected ideas or combining materials in unique ways is also fundamental to creative and imaginative thinking, and the more opportunity children have to make links and connections as they play outside the more challenging and imaginative their play is likely to be. Again, arrangement of space can invite children to make connections.

Elevated spaces

Too often, play areas are literally and metaphorically 'flat' with horizons rarely rising above a metre. Everything fits in to this space. However, height can transform play, perspectives and even relationships as the normal order of things is reversed, and children look down on adults and adults look up to children. To change level is to change perspective and see the world through a different angled lens. Height opens up vistas, and it becomes possible to see over fences and into other spaces that are not accessible to those on the ground. High places can also provide convenient vantage points for children to watch others without feeling conspicuous, and can provide private places for children to be alone or to watch others. They are also identified as popular social places for children to meet and talk (Burke 2005).

Height adds excitement, exhilaration, and feelings of power and control—the 'I'm the king of the castle' effect. Stephenson (2002) identified height as featuring in children's perceptions of scariness, thereby adding to excitement and challenge. Experiencing height also develops mathematical concepts of height, space, distance and perspective.

Height can be designed into play areas through the building of mounds and hills, through trees, tree houses and fixed equipment with high platforms. Alternative access routes and exits can allow children with physical disabilities to access high places, but not be exposed to danger. Bridges and aerial walkways, ideally through trees and netted for safety, if necessary, can provide height and make effective use of space at different levels, creating interesting 'underworlds' below.

Wild spaces

Few children growing up in urban landscapes experience wildness yet young children seem drawn to wild places. Moore makes a powerful argument for retaining 'rough ground' in the midst of urban landscapes. He emphasizes the dynamic relationship between the ground and the children's use of it:

The indeterminacy of rough ground allows it to become a play-partner, like other forms of creative partnership: actress-audience, potter-clay, painter-canvas. The exploring/creating child is not making 'art' so much as using the landscape as a medium for understanding the world by continually destructing/reconstructing it.

(Moore 1986: 242)

This concept of landscape as a play partner is an important one. Adults frequently see wild spaces as unkempt, uncontrolled, undesirable and unsafe, but children can see wild spaces as offering freedom to control their own play to create, construct, deconstruct and transform. The relationship between landscape and play is reciprocal and dynamic. Features of the landscape suggest play themes, for example, a mound becomes a mountain to be climbed or a tree with spreading branches becomes an octopus (Waller 2006).

Wild and rough, rather than caged and manicured spaces allow more scope for the imagination, for being creative, for exploring a world of living things and for developing a sense of place. A wild area exposes children to the unexpected and the unpredictable, and can conjure excitement, mystery and a sense of adventure. Moving through long grass and bushes that reach above children's heads can be equivalent to adults navigating a tangled jungle, and patches of unmown grass can make exciting places to explore (Figure 4.3). Herrington (2005a) describes how a group of children staged a fierce protest when a favourite play area of long grass was about to be mowed indicating that this was an important place for them.

Areas of 'suggested' wildness, such as fallen trees, boulders, long grass, tangled vines, a thicket of bamboo can offer valuable sites for exploration, adventure, imagination and sheer sensory pleasure:

To a child there is more joy in a rubbish tip than a flowering rockery, in a fallen tree than a piece of statuary, in a muddy track than a gravel path ... Yet the cult among his elders is to trim, to pave, to smooth out, to clean up, to prettify, to convert to economic advantage as if the maximum utilisation of surrounding amenities has become a line of poetry.

(Opie and Opie 1969: 13)

Although Iona and Peter Opie were writing in the 1960s, their argument is as relevant today with the 'designerification' of domestic and public gardens, and the popularity of instant garden 'make-overs', which usually provide little scope for children's play.

Figure 4.3 Moving through long grass and bushes that reach above children's heads can be equivalent to adults navigating a tangled jungle.

Spaces for exploration and investigation

> What is important is '. . . the preparation of a provocative environment where new chances are made possible'.
>
> (McMillan 1930:78)

A provocative environment is one that offers interest and surprise, invites curiosity and exploration, and has infinite possibility. Materials such as earth, sand and water provide endless opportunities for play and exploration (Wood 1993). The sand and water area in Figure 4.4 includes a fountain for exploring strong jets of water. The space can be used for paddling, but a convenient plug allows the water to be drained when children and adults wish. The water can flow into the sand area allowing new connections and 'chances' to be made. Sand can be moulded, shaped and transformed by children, but offers surprises when it dries, changing colour and texture, and providing new opportunities for play. Nearby planting is carefully planned to stimulate the senses, including smell, sound and touch, and bushes are positioned to move and rustle in the wind, to create dappled light effects and so on.

A rich variety of sensory stimuli invite young children to explore and investigate, and every part of the environment can offer rich sensory experiences. For example, the hard pathways for vehicles and wheeled toys in Figure 4.5 have been transformed into places to explore texture not just with the hands and eyes, but also with the ears and the whole body as sounds and vibrations change as wheels pass over the different surfaces.

In a provocative environment children will find and pursue their own challenges. I watched a two-year-old spend a long time trying to fix a clothes peg to a thistle. He was fascinated by the prickly sensa-

Figure 4.4 A sand and water play area, a space offering rich sensory experiences and provocations.

Figure 4.5 Textured paths and surfaces provide an interesting 'soundscape' as children ride over them.

tion. His fingers recoiled, but he kept returning to the self-imposed challenge. In another setting, two children tried to use a bucket to 'catch' water from a small bubbling fountain (Figure 4.6). It proved too difficult. They solved the problem by using a length of pipe to transfer water from the fountain to the bucket. It required considerable collaboration, coordination and perseverance to succeed. The environment was provocative. It invited them to explore but it was also problematic and challenging:

Figure 4.6 A provocative environment offers new possibilities and problems to solve.

> The child's mode of being in the world is such that the world becomes an invitation. It is things in the beckoning world that invite the child, that awakens his curiosity, that invoke . . . him to make sense of that multitude of experiences lying beyond; in short to become, through his play, both an actor and a meaning maker.
>
> (Polakow 1992: 39)

Spaces of mystery and enchantment

Young children are avid observers, often fascinated by minute details, shades of colour, intricate patterns, shifting light and shadow. Some of the taken-for-granted things in the environment can be a source of mystery and delight for young children. For example, the play of light through leaves, moving shadows, a disappearing rain puddle or slowly melting ice can evoke wonder and curiosity. Alex, aged three, watched a patch of ice melting and exclaimed 'look, look it's melting into the magic'.

The sense of wonder that accompanies the mysterious is fundamental to many aspects of learning as Einstein has argued:

> The most beautiful thing we can experience is the mysterious. It is the source of all true art and science. He to whom this

emotion is a stranger, who can no longer pause to wonder and stand rapt in awe is as good as dead; his eyes are closed.

(Einstein 1984: 27)

Opportunities for experiencing mystery and beauty will be found in any rich environment, but they also need to be planned for. For example, understanding how light and shadow work in the play area, creating spaces where children can experience shadow and darkness, designing coloured glass portholes or peepholes in walls to catch the sun and create rainbow effects, designing planting to provide dappled, moving light or bushes, which rustle in the wind are all examples of how the design of the environment can foster a sense of beauty, mystery and wonder.

Natural spaces

When they have a choice it appears that children prefer natural environments to play in (Moore 1986; Titman 1994). Armitage (1999) researched children's perceptions of playgrounds in Hull and found that while equipment initially attracted children to playgrounds it was the natural features, such as grass, flowers, trees, shrubs, bushes and trees, which children rated highly and sustained the play for longer. Often these features had been provided only to soften the environment and provide aesthetic value, but to children they afforded rich play opportunities.

Too often nature is used as a space filling or decorative feature of play areas. Plants are packed into walled beds or concrete tubs, and if maintained by contract gardeners can be ripped out at regular intervals and replaced by new instantly flowering varieties. Nature then becomes little more than a scenic backdrop, rather than the setting or stage for play. Contrast this with a Children's Centre in Surrey, England, which created a wild garden environment for children in the centre of an urban housing estate:

We wanted our children and families to absorb into the fibre of their very being the natural world, its beauty, its wild life, the changes of the seasons, and to be aware of the response of the environment and ourselves to weather. We wanted families to see plants dancing in the lightest wind, to feel stormy weather blowing their hair, hear rain pattering on leaves, smell the damp ground, to see light shining on foliage and how it changes the garden hour by hour, day by day.

(Robinson 2006: 1)

The Centre includes woodlands, fields of long grass, flowering meadows, and an abundance of trees and bushes. There are pathways meandering through wild areas, living willow dens, tunnels and fences. The garden is full of wild life, with caterpillars and butterflies, foxes and badgers to name but a few. Children see footprints in the sandpit and quietly watch the duck sitting on her eggs in the long grass. They can paddle in rock pools, operate jets of water from a fountain and create streams that flow down to the sandpit.

Here, nature is the context to the play it is not merely decorative. When children are involved with nature, rather than passive observers a deeper and longer-lasting relationship can be established. One way children can become intimately acquainted with nature is through gardening where they are active in digging, planting, watering and harvesting.

A design for children's play area therefore needs to include digging patches and children's gardens where children and adults can grow vegetables, fruit, flowers, herbs and spices. The design of children's gardens is important and, as Froebel argued, small plots for one or two children ensure that children are really active in the process of gardening and see the results of their own, rather than someone else's actions. Plots of land that are subdivided into smaller plots by dividing paths or stepping stones allow children to garden without stepping on planted areas. Low surrounding walls are useful for sitting or kneeling on or placing plants or tools. Some higher level beds enable children or adults in wheel chairs or those unable to bend down, to garden at a height where close eye contact can be maintained. A nearby tap and hose pipe, and storage area for gardening tools is needed so that children can be independent in watering and finding the tools to dig. Transparent compost bins allow children to experience the cycle of growth and decay and regeneration.

Small ponds, bird tables and nesting boxes, damp and dark places with logs or boulders to provide habitats for small insects and amphibians are all ways that nature can be experienced first hand in a real context.

I remember planning a new outdoor play area for children. As a staff team we spent days searching for plants, shrubs and trees which would provide interest and sensory pleasure. For example, we looked for plants with leaves and flowers offering interesting textures, colours, patterns, scents or tastes like lemon balm and mint but also plants with names rich in metaphor and symbolic meaning such as lamb's ears, bleeding hearts, cowslips, shepherd's purse and old man's beard (Figure 4.7).

We also looked for plants that would provide a range of different

Figure 4.7 Plants can delight the senses with new scents, patterns, colours and textures.

'props' for play such as seed heads, interesting bark, textured leaves. Over many years it was fascinating to see how such plants have been used for play. The leaves of lemon balm were regularly picked for mixing with water and creating 'lemonade', mint leaves were used for medicine and, when squeezed, the resulting green liquid became 'poison'. Honesty seeds were used for money, treasure or food. Tough grass stems were threaded with petals to make necklaces and bamboo stems became fishing rods or light sabres. Lavender flowers and rose petals were mixed with water for perfume and petals, seeds, twigs and stones were used for pattern and picture making (Figure 4.8). These are just a few examples of the infinite variety of ways in which plants became props for play. Children attended to certain features of the plant or flower, its hollow stem, scent, hairy stem or soft texture, seeing its symbolic potential. Moore researched children's use of plant props and identified that:

> Plant parts provided irresistible sensory gems, pinpoints of colour, smell and geometric form that focused children's attention and set the wheels of their imagination in motion.
>
> (Moore 1989: 4)

Figure 4.8 Petals, leaves, seeds, twigs, logs and stones can be used for pattern and picture making.

Natural processes

Children's experience and understanding of nature can also be enhanced if the play area is designed with materials that can draw attention to natural features, such as wind, rain, shadow, snow, ice, fog, and forces, such as gradient and gravity. Young children are endlessly curious about features of the natural world as can be seen in the surprised expression of a toddler touching snow for the first time or the persistent questions of four-year-olds such as 'where does the water go when I pull the plug?'; will it make a flood downstairs? *(said by a flat dweller watching water flow down an outdoor drain).*

Transparent guttering and down pipes, above ground rainwater run-offs, ditches and drainage systems can enable children to see more clearly what happens to rainwater, and simultaneously provide spaces where they can dig channels, create dams and explore the flow of water. Play space is then transformed by heavy rain. A water pump linked to rain water storage can provide opportunities for children to explore suction, forces and cause and effect and begin to see the relationship or what Athey (1990: 70) terms 'functional dependency' between the movement of the handle, and the amount and flow of the water. Water wheels encourage exploration of the force of water, rotation, cause and effect, and the relationship between the force of water and the speed of rotation.

One nursery setting included a weather vane, a small windmill and wind chimes hanging from trees. These drew children's attention to the force, direction and movement of air and wind and provoked questions such as 'where does the wind go at night time? Does it go in the trees?' 'What's that noise? Is it the wind talking to the trees?' The wind also became a feature of imaginative play 'I'm the wind and I'm going to blow you over with my magic power!'.

Herrington outlines how an outdoor environment for young children can be designed to allow children to experience these physical processes, as well as create interesting spaces for play and at the same time create a sustainable landscape (Herrington 2005a).

Space for the imagination

Open-ended and anything-you-want-it-to-be spaces

Space that is full of potential, rather than full of equipment, allows children to act on the environment, rather than to respond to its pre-existing design. It allows them to create their own places for play. Research by Broadhead (2004), although focusing on indoor play suggests that the 'anything you want it to be' spaces compared with the pre-prepared themed play areas promote complex social interaction as they allow children to negotiate and develop their own play themes. She noted that the open-ended play also promoted high levels of affectionate physical contact and new dimensions of friendship. There was more laughter and joyfulness as children engaged with the themes of the play. Frequently children initiated and sustained themes that had elements of fear, danger and threat, such as the 'dark cave', 'dead chicken' or 'roller coaster', themes, which are unlikely to appear on adults' planning sheets!

The 'anything you want it to be' principle also applies to the provision of any fixed play structures. The issue of fixed versus flexible resources outdoors is still a controversial one with designers offering play equipment depicting items, such as trains, aeroplanes, boats, castles or themed resources based on, say, the seaside or a children's story such as Peter Pan. As Bilton (2002) points out such structures frequently stretch the designer's imaginations more than the child's. Yet such is the power of children's imaginations that they do transform even the most realistic looking structure into something other than it is meant to be. Michael Laris, a playground designer, describes how observations of children using his recently designed castle provided a salutary lesson:

> [I watched them lift up the drawbridge lever arm of the castle as] they shouted 'anchors up—we're sailing'.
>
> Sailing? My castle, sailing? Here I learned an important lesson—it is not the designer who decides how a thing will ultimately be used. It is the children who decide . . . This observation made clear to me the crucial need for designs that are less obvious, more abstract and include a diversity of shapes and materials so that they are open to a wide range of imaginative interpretations.
>
> (Laris 2005: 16)

Open-ended, abstract, with a diversity of shapes and materials seem key principles that might underpin resources for children's play. As we examined in Chapter 2, the essential element is that it is the children who transform, rather than the adults who pre-form (Drummond 1999). Spaces that are open-ended, transformable with plenty of movable or 'loose' parts can provide space for creativity and imagination to flourish (Figure 4.9).

Figure 4.9 Spaces that are open-ended, transformable with plenty of movable, loose parts can provide space for creativity and imagination to flourish.

Loose parts

Over thirty years ago, Simon Nicholson, son of artist Ben Nicholson and sculptor Barbara Hepworth, outlined his theory of 'loose parts' arguing that 'in any environment, both the degree of inventiveness and creativity and the possibility of discovery are directly linked to the number and kind of variables in it.' He argued that environments that do not work in human terms, including many schools and play-grounds, do not meet the loose parts criteria. Architects and builders have all the fun with designs and materials. However, Nicholson argues, the fun and creativity have been stolen from children and the resulting environments are 'clean, static and impossible to play around with' (Nicholson 1971: 30–34).

An outdoor environment needs to have a multitude of loose parts such as logs, small boulders, plant materials, or building materials, such as blocks, crates, boxes, ladders, planks, tyres, tarpaulins, blan-kets and so on for transforming. In this way, children can construct and create their own environments. The children in Figure 4.10 spent a whole morning building a den from milk crates, planks and fabrics. They subdivided the space into kitchen, living room and bedroom then covered the space with blankets so that the inside was dark.

Imaginative play using 'loose parts' or 'props' helps children to make connections and to develop possibility thinking, the essence of creative thought. Froebel argued that 'as the play material becomes

Figure 4.10 Children building a den from milk crates, planks and fabrics.

less tangible so there is a greater advance in creative expression' (Lilley 1967: 113) and this can be seen in the following example:

> A group of 5 year olds (girls and boys) spent a good hour making 'mud pies' in the playhouse but the sand to make them was brought in a paper bag from the sand pit, the water from the fountain, the fruit (sawdust) from the 'arena' where sawing had been done, the frosting was shaken from an old can of cleaning powder. It should be noted that this is an excellent illustration of how important minute parts of the manipulative environment can be for imaginative play.
>
> (Allen of Hurtwood 1968: 77)

It also illustrates the importance of an environment that supports children making connections, and collecting and combining their materials from a wide area.

Dens and refuges

The desire to create small, intimate, private places seems to be a characteristic of childhood and features in children's play in a range of different countries and cultures. (Moore 1986; Sobel 2002; Kylin 2003). Children create their own secret places, known variously as bush houses, cubbies, dens, forts or camps often in undefined, 'in between' and 'left over' spaces. These small, secret, worlds are calm, ordered and reassuringly secure. They allow for privacy, imagination and temporary ownership, and are important ways that children can feel a sense of agency in shaping and creating their own special place, making their mark on the world. In this way, children transform space into place or as Edith Cobb claimed 'make a world in which to find a place to discover a self' (Cobb, cited in Sobel 1990).

While den making seems to be a particular feature of middle childhood, a similar desire to inhabit small nest like spaces can also be found in early childhood. Kirby (1989) mapped the behaviour of 26 preschoolers and found that they spent over half their time in three small refuge spaces that occupied only a small part of the total area available to them. She identified that richer and more complex dramatic play took place in dens that had a ceiling effect, which had a number of sub-spaces loosely connected, with different entry and exit points, and which were visually connected to the wider surroundings. Kirby's research identified that a significant feature of dens is to be able to see out, but remain concealed from view. Manufactured dens such as little houses are rarely used for such a purpose as the space is too open and interrupted. It is the act of creating and occupying the space that is important. The current trend for adult directed den building activities cuts across such research evidence and seems an intrusion into these secret places of childhood.

Bushes, trees with low lying branches such as weeping willow, clearings in densely planted areas, secret niches, space behind sheds, can provide the necessary space for children to create and build their own dens and hideaways. This often means planning ahead and planting bushes with dens and hiding spaces in mind. For example, laurel bushes were deliberately planted in a circle to create the den in Figure 4.11. The play in such a den is considerably enriched by the 'plasticity' of the environment, and by the plentiful supply of props or loose parts such as twigs, leaves and flowers. The children are using leaves to stand for pizza and stones to stand for eggs.

This opportunity to create one's own secret place in homes, gardens or local neighbourhoods is severely reduced in urban areas. Designer houses, flats and gardens take little account of this aspect of children's play and the small spaces, such as under the stairs, in the basement or in cupboards under the eaves, which feature so strongly in adult memories of play have all but been eliminated as the utility of space is maximized, forcing children to resort to less versatile spaces under bunk beds, in clothes cupboards or in the stair wells of blocks

Figure 4.11 Space for the imagination. Laurel bushes have been planted in a circle to create a den, with a plentiful supply of 'props', such as twigs, leaves, flowers and stones.

of flats. This makes it even more important that outdoor space offers the space and potential for children to be den builders and place makers:

> If we allow children to shape their own world in childhood, then they will grow up knowing and feeling that they can participate in shaping the big world tomorrow.
>
> (Sobel 2002: 161)

Spaces for movement

Movement such as we have seen in Chapter 2 is fundamental to young children's well being and learning. Margaret McMillan argued that:

> Children need space at all ages. But from the age of one to seven, space, that is ample space, is almost as much wanted as food and air. To move, to run, to find things out by new movement, to feel ones' life in every limb, that is the life of early childhood.
>
> (McMillan 1930: 11)

'Feeling ones' life in every limb' requires space. Yet too often space is filled up, cluttered with equipment, over designed and organized, leaving little room for children to fly through the air as an aeroplane or superhero, jump as frogs or chase imaginary robbers. This requires open space and young children need to experience the vastness of open space, as well as the more intimate secluded and sheltered space.

It is the diversity of movement opportunities that is important. Flat play areas with a single climbing frame offer limited scope for movement. Instead play areas should offer opportunities for a wide range of movements in a range of different situations. For example, crawling, lying, rolling, twisting, turning, lifting, sliding, swinging, balancing, punching, pouncing, hitting, throwing, climbing, walking, skipping, hopping, hanging.

While some smooth ground is important, rough terrain is important too. Research by Fjortoft (2001) has shown that uneven ground can develop children's balance and coordination. Some wild terrain where children can crawl under low branches, climb over fallen tree trunks, balance on or jump off tree stumps, jump in puddles, clamber through fallen leaves, negotiate a muddy track or slide down a grassy bank provides diverse movement opportunities. Undulating and weaving paths and stepping stones also require controlled movements. Small bridges or board walks can traverse uneven ground providing alternative routes for children using wheeled chairs or walkers, and can provide additional hiding places below.

Upper torso strength and agility can be developed through bars for hanging, ropes for swinging, ladders for climbing, and slides or planks for pulling and sliding. Objects for dragging, pulling and pushing are important with pulley ropes for lifting and transporting heavy weights. Open flat space for kicking, throwing, hitting and rolling balls is also important.

The close relationship between movement and conceptual development and the work of Athey (1990) on schemas would suggest that opportunities are needed for children to move **horizontally**, **vertically**, **diagonally**, to **encircle**, go **through** tunnels, **over** and **under** bridges, **along** planks, **in between** boulders, to hide **inside** small enclosures, to **cross boundaries** and so on.

Space for stillness

However, space for quietness and stillness is as important as space for noise and movement. Young children often choose outdoors as a place for solitude, for quiet companionship or as a place for reflective dreaming. Nature itself invites quiet contemplation or intense fascination, and it is not unusual to see children outdoors silent and still as they watch a snail or gaze at clouds moving in the sky. Time for dreaming, it could be argued, is slowly disappearing from children's ever more organized and entertained lives. Yet, as Bachelard suggests, it is paradoxically often in quiet stillness that our minds wander freely into a world, which is no longer restricted by physical spatial boundaries, but only the limits of our imagination:

> As soon as we become motionless we are elsewhere, we are dreaming in a world which is immense. Indeed, immensity is the movement of the motionless man. It is one of the dynamic characteristics of quiet daydreaming.
>
> (Bachelard 1994: 184)

Small semi-secluded areas, seats, comfortable grassy spaces to sit or to lie, hammocks, swinging seats can provide quiet places, where children can be still, dream, watch and find quiet intimacy with others.

Social and intimate spaces

> The most precious gift we can give to the young is social space, the necessary space—or privacy—in which to become human beings.
>
> (Opie and Opie 1959: 16)

A key concept underpinning design in the nursery centres in Reggio Emilia, Italy is 'relational space' that is how the space promotes relationships between children and between children and adults (Ceppi and Zini 1999). Different spatial arrangements can lead to different interactions and relationships. Smaller spaces, circular hollows or enclosures, spaces between or behind bushes, spaces under bridges, and canopies over hiding holes or barrels for example are rich spaces for friendships to flourish often because they are secret, partially hidden and therefore rich places for pretence.

Seating offers spaces for rest, talk and interaction (Figure 4.12). Seating which faces inwards encourages greater communication and interaction, whereas seating facing outwards, such as that around a tree provides opportunities for children to sit and watch others (although in my experience such seating is used less for sitting and, instead, becomes a resource for play and a good place for circular

Figure 4.12 Seating offers space for rest, talk and interaction. It also provides hiding places underneath.

running and exploring the interesting phenomena of 'being in front' and then 'being behind').

Far from being a passive activity, observing is an important strategy children use to learn about play and to eventually gain access to the play and build friendships. Indeed, as Rubin's research suggests, successful players are those who are sensitive to the themes, roles and characters of the play having previously 'tuned in' by observing (Rubin 1983). Design of play areas should therefore include social spaces where children can observe alongside play areas. Low walls, steps and strategically placed logs can provide suitable 'perching places' for both children and adults.

Intimate spaces for adults and children

Outdoors is not just about adventure and exploration, it is also about closeness and intimacy. It is close and secure relationships that give children the confidence to explore and then return to a trusted adult when needed. Observe toddlers playing outdoors and often they have one eye on a parent or key adult as if to check out 'is this safe for me to explore? Are you looking at what I'm looking at?' Young children are social beings, and need adults who will share their excitement and curiosity who are affectionate, playful and responsive. The design of play areas can support close relationships through the provision of small spaces for adults and children, such as hammocks or swing seats, grass or camomile surfaces to sit or lie on. Spaces for adults to frolic, tumble, play roly poly, peek boo, and generally romp and rummage with children are all important to the development of strong close relationships. Spongy, rubberized surfaces or cold windswept tarmac are not conducive to such intimate, playful interactions.

Fluid spaces

Finally, a well-designed play area should not be fixed and rigid, but should change, evolve, and literally and metaphorically 'grow' as children and adults transform it for their own purposes. Fluid, rather than rigid spaces can ebb and flow in response to the changing landscapes of play. Fluid spaces are not fixed or finished, but are capable of growth and change. Fluid spaces are not confined to the 'here and now', but allow the imagination to cross boundaries of time and space. They allow children and adults to become authors of their own spaces and creators of meaningful places for play.

The most important thing is that structure and form leave the greatest possible space for the future evolution because the real and most important designer of the [play area] should be the collectivity which uses it.

(De Carlo 1997: 107)

How does design shape children's use of space?

Research evidence supports the view that there is a close connection between design and children's play, and use of space, although this is a difficult area to research. Herrington (1997) reports on a project to re-design an outdoor play area of a day care setting for babies and toddlers in Canada. The interdisciplinary project aimed to translate theories of young children's social, emotional and sensorimotor development into landscape forms, textures and images, drawing on theories of experience, order, harmony, sacredness and place found in landscape theory.

The design of the infant garden included a central mounded ring with sand in the centre for digging, dumping, rolling, forming and patting. The ring provided a sense of enclosure, a communal space connected to other areas, and also gave a sense of mystery and challenge as infants navigated their way over it to reach the other side. The shade structure over the sand pit was designed to catch the movement of the wind, and encourage listening and watching. Gardens were arranged in interspersed patches, to promote the development of object permanence and playful encounters. A circle of pine trees offered a rich sensory environment for touching and feeling, as well as cones to play with. A mist field included small child controlled emitters of a fine mist, which encouraged infants to touch, feel and move their bodies.

Research identified that after the transformation of the play area from a flat grass space to a garden, the infants were much more active, made greater use of the whole space and spent less time sitting than in the previous grass-covered yard. Systematic analysis of video footage showed that design features, such as the stepping stones and the mystery behind the grass mound drew the infants out into the garden. Children played more with natural materials and their manipulations were more varied and complex. Significantly, the children were involved in many more play interactions with adults in this re-designed garden (Herrington 1997).

This example illustrates how design of outdoor play space can either enable or constrain children's play and learning. The essential principle is that there should be a close relationship between the design of space, and those elements of children's play and learning that we recognize as being important.

5

GARDENS OR FORESTS?

As we have seen in Chapter 3, the literal and metaphorical notion of the 'garden' has been a distinctive feature of nursery provision. However, in recent years there has been a rapid growth of another form of outdoor provision, the Forest School. The word Forest conjures up a different image, suggesting a wilder, riskier, scarier space, less confined and cultivated than the 'garden'.

Forest School offers a very different landscape for children. Here, children from as young as three years old, accompanied by nursery or school staff, and a Forest School leader, spend half a day a week, sometimes longer, in local woodland areas with little or no shelter, in all weathers. Children play in the woods, climb trees, explore streams and ponds, wade through mud, slide down muddy slopes, build dens and fires, and use real tools, such as saws and knives.

One of the Forest School principles is that it 'builds on an individual's innate motivation and positive attitude to learning, offering them the opportunities to take risks, make choices and initiate learning for themselves'. It also aims to develop children's confidence and self esteem (Doyle 2006).

Playing out of sight of adults

Children are encouraged to roam freely in the woods and to venture out of sight of adults. Before and during their first visits children play the '1, 2, 3—where are you?' game in which the adults hide in nearby bushes and trees and children have to find them by calling out '1, 2, 3—where are you?' The children have to listen carefully to the adults' reply and locate them from sound, rather than sight. This is a fun game, but has a serious purpose too. It gives all the children a strategy to use if they are lost or feel anxious out of sight of others. Helping children to overcome what can be an overwhelming fear of getting lost, is part of the Forest School's emphasis on empowering children, and developing their confidence and feelings of self-efficacy. Children have even been heard calling out the same refrain in supermarket aisles suggesting that the strategy is transferable to other contexts.

Space for imagination

There are no toys and equipment in Forest School; the natural landscape offers the resources and props for play. Children therefore have to use their imaginations to transform features of the environment. The woods themselves, stories and folklore provide inspiration for playing games of wolves, building houses to hide from the wolves, playing fairies and goblins and, in this five-year-old child's imagination, leprechauns:

> One boy was having difficulty holding the imaginary leprechaun in his hand, while trying to put on his woolly hat. I suggested that maybe he could put the leprechaun into his hat to keep him safe, before putting the hat on his head. He thought about it then told me it would be fine up there 'as leprechauns have so much energy they don't poo or wee'. The idea may have come from having no toilets in the forest!
>
> (Keating 2002)

Children transform features of the environments such as logs, sticks, fir cones, leaves, twigs, and mud into whatever they want them to be. For example, I observed a group of children transform a bush into a house:

> This is our house right?
> Yeah and this is the front door (*pointing to a gap in the bush*)
> Yeah and this can be ring ring! (*making the noise of a bell and pointing to a bump on a nearby tree trunk*)
> No let's say the door's broken and no one's coming in—only Postman Pat letters.
> *The play continued with children pushing letters (leaves) through a small gap in the bushes. Some time later the same gap in the bushes became a hatch for selling ice cream which had been transformed from fir cones.*

Another observation showed children transforming the trunk and roots of a fallen tree into a broken car in need of repair, the dead tree sparking off the idea of a 'broken' car (Figure 5.1).

Transformations

The natural landscape offers children direct first-hand experience of nature so that they can know and come to understand the changing seasons, seeing how a familiar space transforms in sometimes subtle and sometimes dramatic ways. For example, children at the Rising Sun Woodland Pre-School Project experienced how the pond turned from 'an area to play in, to one which had deep bits for my wellies, to an iced over area, to a muddy patch and then finally it no longer existed—"the ice monster had sucked it up with a straw" ' (Proud 1999). Children observe and learn about the natural world, the seasonal changes and begin to respect the laws of nature.

Respect for nature, respect for danger, respect for children

The word 'respect' is very apparent in Forest School literature, respect for the forest environment, respect for nature, respect for the dangers

Figure 5.1 Children transform the trunk and roots of a fallen tree into a broken car in need of repair.

inherent in say fire or water, respect for children and trust that they can with adult support learn to manage risk. Children are not shielded from danger, they don't just watch while adults make fires build shelters or cook food. Rather they are seen as competent with the potential to master skills safely. Gordon Woodall founder of the Bridgwater Forest School in Somerset, England argues:

> It is only when you restrict children from using 'dangerous' things that you get accidents. How can a child respect a fire when he or she is never allowed near it?
>
> (Woodall, cited in McConville 1997: 17)

Making fires

Fire is a significant first-hand experience for children at Forest School, one that they are unlikely to experience in their everyday lives. Children help to make fires by collecting wood. They are encouraged to find, say, five sticks as long as their arm and as thick as their finger. They are shown how to listen carefully to the different snap sounds in order to distinguish live from dead wood. As they search for sticks for cooking food on they look for bendy sticks that will not burn. When they want to transport long branches they realize the need to collaborate and help each other.

Fire is an exciting sensory experience. The sounds of crackling wood, the smell of the smoke or burning wood, the sight of flames dancing or smoke curling are powerful experiences. Fire is both captivating and scary. Through experiencing fire children learn about transformations, about the difference between steam and smoke, the effect of heat on cooking ingredients, such as marshmallows or bread (Figure 5.2). They see the impact that water has on a fire and collect the charcoal to use later for drawing. They learn about the dangers of fire and relate this to their own experiences at home.

Children are taught the necessary skills to be safe. For example, they are taught how to approach a fire, never to turn their backs on it and so on. Skills of whittling wood with a sharp knife are taught in a one-to-one situation with the adult teaching how to hold the knife, and the movements and angle necessary to keep the blade away from the body (Figure 5.3). Children also learn about safe ways of using tools as they see adults using real tools. There are strong echoes here of Froebel and his 'apprenticeship' model of children learning alongside skilled adults (Lilley 1967).

It would seem ironic that in a society characterized as risk averse, such challenging and potentially risky environments appear to be

Figure 5.2 Fire is an exciting, sensory experience—it is both captivating and sensory.

Figure 5.3 Skills of whittling are taught in a one-to-one situation, with the adult teaching how to hold the knife, and the movements and angle necessary to keep the blade away from the body.

hugely popular with parents, teachers and the wider community. This might reflect the importance placed on establishing effective dialogue with parents, on thorough preparation prior to children's visits and the children's enthusiastic responses to their Forest School experience.

Nostalgic and anachronistic?

Do Forest Schools promote a nostalgic, romantic vision of an idealized childhood, which has little relevance to children growing up in a technological society? What use, some might ask, is whittling sticks, making fires or sawing logs to life in the fast lane of twenty-first century urban life? Eva Gullov, a Danish anthropologist, argues that there is a 'touch of nostalgia' about forest kindergartens (Gullov 2003: 28). Drawing on her ethnographic study of forty Danish kindergartens, she argues that there is considerable ambiguity and uncertainty in thinking about children, and where they should be placed. 'Children are separated from their parents, separated from adult life in general, separated from city life and bussed out to another societal vision.'

She questions the pedagogical aims of the forest kindergartens and the relevance of activities such as making fires, building huts or making jam to preparing children for school, or for their future lives as adults, suggesting that these activities properly belong to a bygone age.

> The connection with nature, the association with other kinds of societies tied more closely with earlier forms of livelihood production, can be interpreted as a way of negating the conditions of childhood today, not as some kind of repression but as a political standpoint, an active voice in the discussion of where to place small children. *Carried to its extreme, children should be in childhood, and childhood has no place in modern society.*
> (Gullov 2003: 28 my emphasis)

Gullov is referring here to Danish society; one that it could be argued has a clearer vision of what makes a 'good' childhood. The ambiguities and uncertainties about childhood and places for children are more pronounced in the UK where children are seen as vulnerable, on the one hand, in need of protection including almost constant surveillance, and on the other hand, self-managing, competent individuals capable of learning about and managing risk. The fact that children are bussed away from their everyday lives and communities to secret locations that are fenced as much to keep 'strangers' out as to keep children in, so that they can experience freedoms and opportunities that were once perceived as an integral part of childhood itself does represent some ambiguity. From this perspective, it could be argued that Forest Schools are increasingly marginalizing children from society by removing them from mainstream life without addressing why so few of these opportunities are available to children in other spheres of their lives.

'Learning through', as well as 'learning about'

However, Gullov's suggestion that Forest Schools are somewhat nostalgic and anachronistic is, I would argue, failing to understand the essence of what the Forest School movement is trying to achieve and the pedagogical principles that underpin it. First, the curriculum is not just learning *about* building fires or shelters, or climbing trees, but learning *through* these experiences. Forest Schools are about developing confidence, resilience, independence and interdependence. For example, learning to overcome fears of being lost or out of sight, and having strategies to know what to do is hugely empowering to children compared with learning never to venture out of sight of an adult as they have to learn in other environments, for example, shopping malls. Climbing trees requires some caution and a sense of wariness—is this branch strong enough to take my weight? (Figure 5.4) Pulling another child out of the mud or moving a large log is about collaboration and teamwork; cooking on a fire is about learning cause and effect, managing risk and taking some responsibility for your own actions. The power of the imagination brings twenty-first century life into the woodlands as a clearing in the woods becomes a space station or a tree stump becomes a rocket launch pad.

Resilience and resourcefulness

Secondly, Gullov's perspective illustrates the tension between the 'todayness' of childhood and the 'tomorrowness' of their future schooling and lives. However, if there is one thing we can predict about life in the twenty-first century, it is that it will be uncertain and unpredictable, fast moving and fast changing, requiring people who are flexible, adaptable, innovative and creative. Learning to deal with uncertainty, 'knowing what to do when you don't know what to do' (Claxton 1999: 11) having the confidence to try things without fear of making mistakes, overcoming fears, and developing resilience and resourcefulness would appear to be essential elements of a toolkit of

Figure 5.4 Climbing trees requires caution and wariness. Is this branch strong enough to take my weight?

learning. The Forest School environment, far from being nostalgic, outdated, romantic, is, I would argue, entirely appropriate in developing healthy, competent, resilient, resourceful, imaginative children fit for an uncertain and unpredictable world.

Is there any evidence?

Research on Forest Schools in the UK is thin, but evaluation studies suggest that Forest Schools can have a significant impact on children's well being and development.

A study by Murray and O'Brien (2005: 6) indicated that children attending Forest Schools showed:

- increased confidence;
- better ability to work collaboratively;
- increased awareness of the consequences of their actions;
- improved motivation and concentration;
- improved physical stamina;
- increased understanding of and respect for the environment.

These findings were from an action research project using a self-appraisal methodology, as well as individual child tracking. It is, of course, difficult to identify the specific contribution that participation in Forest School might have made to these aspects of children's development. Nevertheless, the study provides evidence of the very positive perceptions of children, parents and practitioners to the Forest School experience, and of the possible impact on children's lives and learning. Significantly the research found that it was not just children who gained from the experience, but practitioners and parents too. The practitioners gained new perspectives and understanding of the children as they observed them in a very different context. This led to closer and more trusting relationships between children and adults. There was also a ripple effect beyond the Forest School as children brought their experiences and interests home, and for example, asked parents to take them out to woodlands at weekends.

Evidence from Norwegian nature kindergartens

Further evidence comes from research in Norway where nature kindergartens or *barnhaeger* are an established part of provision for young children, and where children from three to six may spend all or much of the day playing outside in a forest playscape. Research by Grahn on the impact of these natural environments on children's play suggests that in comparison with conventional playgrounds the play was more complex, creative and social, with more mixed age and gender groupings. Relationships between children were improved with fewer conflicts. Researchers also found that children who played in these environments had improved motor fitness and lower rates of absence because of sickness (Grahn, cited in Fjortoft 2004).

In a systematic year-long study, Fjortoft compared a group of children in a natural forest environment with those in a constructed environment with more conventional equipment, such as swings sandpit, seesaw, slide and climbing houses. Using the EUROFIT European test of Physical Fitness (Adam *et al*, cited in Fjortoft 2004) she compared the motor development of the two groups of children and found that those using the forest environment made more rapid gains in all areas of motor ability, and there were significant differences between the two groups of children in tests on balance, coordination, strength and agility.

Fjortoft (2001) suggests that the dynamic and rough natural playscapes offer more challenge to children and require greater versatility of movement leading to improved motor development. The unpredictability of the forest environment with its uneven terrain, obstacles to manoeuvre over and under, varying climbing heights, affords children more opportunities to test their limits, to use their bodies in a wider range of movements than in a conventional more predictable playground environment. For example, climbing a tree requires dexterity to adjust to the different spaces between branches. It requires some caution and a temporary stillness, while fine pressure is exerted to test the strength of a branch. It requires adjustment of body movement to squeeze through, over, under and in between irregular branches. A fixed climbing frame on the other hand offers only regular defined spaces between bars. It is entirely predictable. As the Danish landscape architect Helle Nebelong argued:

> When the distance between all the rungs on the climbing net or the ladder is exactly the same, the child has no need to concentrate on where he puts his feet. This lesson cannot be carried over into all the knobbly and asymmetrical forms with which one is confronted throughout life.
>
> (Nebelong 2004: 30)

Challenging play opportunities

The Forest landscape offered challenging play experiences that changed according to the seasons. For example, the winter snow and ice provided sliding slopes with differing degrees of challenge, as can be seen in Figure 5.5 'The children made high-speed competitions in different sliding disciplines: on their backs, on their stomachs, feet first, head first, and so on' (Fjortoft 2001: 14). The dense snow layer made the trees more accessible for climbing (Figure 5.6), but also provided opportunities for building play houses and dens, and for making snow figures.

Fjortoft states without comment that the children, aged from five to seven, spent from one to two hours every day in these challenging environments, which lay outside the kindergarten fence. Children were free to explore the areas closest to the kindergarten, but had to be accompanied by adults to access the further parts. It is inconceivable that children in the UK would be able to play freely and out of sight of adults in such challenging environments, including deep snow, and this reflects the very different cultural perceptions of childhood, play and risk. Norwegian kindergartens appear to place a high value on challenging and creative play and have high expectations of children's ability to master physical skills.

Figure 5.5 Winter snow and ice provides sliding slopes with differing degrees of challenge.

Underpinning values are crucial

While the Forest environment is rich in potential, it is how it is used by children and adults that matter. The ethos and values that underpin its use are therefore fundamental. In this sense, the Forest School movement is about much more than children's landscapes and play-

Figure 5.6 A dense snow layer makes the trees more accessible for climbing.

scapes; it is about a view of children and childhood that sees children as competent, capable, curious, adventurous and imaginative. The Norwegian nature kindergartens appear to place more emphasis on imaginative, creative and collaborative play whereas the Forest Schools in the UK appear to place more emphasis on identifying curriculum potential outdoors. Even the names 'school' and 'kindergarten' suggest different emphases. Crucially, it is the underpinning values that are central. After all, Forest Schools *could* be places where children are led around on nature walks with didactic lessons on identifying the flora and fauna, and instruction not to wander out of sight of adults. Such use would obviously reflect very different assumptions about children and about pedagogy.

What can we learn from Forest Schools?

It could be argued that many of the distinctive features of Forest Schools are part of a long-standing tradition of nursery education and care, and progressive schooling, and are not necessarily 'new'. However, as Moss and Petrie point out, to the extent that we are restating views 'we are doing so at a particular point in history, with its own characteristic social organisation, which furnishes a new and distinct site for rethinking the relationship between children and society' (Moss and Petrie 2002: 132). I would argue that Forest Schools can offer contemporary children the wild open spaces, contact with nature and opportunity for learning about and managing risk that are denied them in other aspects of their lives.

Although the Forest school movement in the UK is growing, children's access to a forest environment remains limited and varies according to region. Temporal access is also restricted as, unlike the nature kindergartens in Denmark and Norway, children have access only once a week for half a day. There is a real danger that Forest schools can be seen as compensatory—offering children a taste of something that is not available to them in other aspects of their lives. There is also a danger that experiences at Forest Schools offer conflicting experiences from those that children have in their schools or nurseries. Students on the BA Early Childhood Studies programme at Roehampton University visiting Forest Schools often note that there can be a sharp contrast between the ethos of the Forest School, and the sometimes impoverished and unchallenging outdoor play environments of the children's base school or nursery.

While it is paramount to maintain the uniqueness of the Forest school environments, we also need to focus closely on what we can learn from them:

- Forest Schools underline the importance of environments which broaden children's first-hand experience and provide opportunities of learning in a real context, which makes sense.
- They raise expectations of what young children are able to do, given appropriate guidance and confirm the importance of a view of children as competent. Nursery Schools have long argued that young children can safely learn to use real tools such as woodwork

and gardening tools as did the adventure playground movement in the 1950s and 1960s (Allen of Hurtwood 1968).

- They show that wild and natural landscapes with varying terrains can promote rich imaginative and creative play, as children transform features of the landscape and natural found materials. Children do not necessarily need predetermined equipment and toys.
- Environments do not have to be fine tuned to a particular age group, but children will take from an environment that which is particularly relevant, challenging or interesting to them.
- With appropriate clothing and enthusiastic adults children enjoy and learn from all weathers and all seasons. There is no such thing as bad weather.
- Through immersion in nature children can, with adult support and guidance learn to respect nature, develop an understanding of their own place in the natural world and begin to appreciate the interconnectedness of living things.

If Forest Schools are to become more than a transitory feature of only some children's lives then we need to look at how elements of the Forest School experience can become a part of children's experience in a wide range of different settings. This means learning from and adapting the principles underpinning the Forest School movement, and considering how natural play spaces and opportunities for risk and challenge can become integral parts of *all* outdoor play environments for young children, particularly for those who have to spend their time on spongy rubber safety surfaces, playing with plastic toys inches from the ground.

Forest nurseries

Rather than taking children 'out' to Forest environments maybe we could learn from the Scandinavian model of locating nurseries 'in' such environments. A recent initiative in Scotland, for example, involves a childminder, with help from a lottery grant, setting up Britain's first open air nursery located in a wood. The 'Secret Garden' nursery will, when it opens, have 'none of the games and equipment seen in a normal suburban nursery: plastic see-saws, cushioned vinyl floors, sterilised building blocks. The curriculum will be devoted to nature walks, rearing chickens, climbing trees, mud play and vegetable gardening. Their playground will be the forest and their shelter a wattle and daub "cob" building with outdoor toilets' (Carrell 2006). But how, one wonders, would children experience and learn to value the built environment; days out in city schools?

It seems that the metaphor of 'forest' as an environment for young children is a growing phenomenon and one that challenges the many manufactured, sanitized, plasticized environments that have emerged in the last decade. The forest, I would argue, should be encouraged to grow and encroach on some of the garden so that the wilder, more challenging and riskier aspects of the forest become an integral part of the philosophy underpinning the nursery garden.

6

PLAYING OUTDOORS: RISK AND CHALLENGE

There is always a certain risk to being alive and if you are more alive there is more risk.

(Ibsen)

Some of my most powerful memories of playing outside as a child are of doing scary things like plucking up courage to go down the damp, dark, semi-derelict air raid shelter, or choosing to climb the tree with the bendiest branches or placing pennies on the railway line and proudly parading the squashed coins as proof of 'daring'. One powerful memory of the winter of 1962 involved taking the sledge up to the highest, steepest slope and sliding down at an exhilarating speed. Before each slide we feigned mock terror and engaged in the ritual of choosing the flowers for our funerals, this was, after all, so dangerous that we could die! In reality, we felt on the borderline of safe and unsafe. This precarious zone was maintained and when the game became a little too safe, we varied our technique adding an extra element of challenge.

I am sure I am not alone in these memories and seminars with students and early years educators typically include many similar examples. What is it that makes children choose to do scary things, to delight in the thrill and excitement of physical challenge or of seemingly danger-defying pursuits? Why do they exaggerate the terror involved and delight in scaring each other even further by hyping up the possible risks and recounting experiences of 'scariness' in days and weeks to come? Unlike the real world, terrifying experiences of childhood these play experiences were deliberately sought and repeated again and again. The more exaggerated the claims to danger the more delight in the play.

Dizzy play

Such play has some resemblance to what Caillois terms *ilynx* or dizzy play, which is characterized by 'an attempt to momentarily destroy the stability of perception and inflict a kind of voluptuous panic upon an otherwise lucid mind' (Caillois 2001: 23). *Ilynx* is the Greek word for whirling water and dizzy play often has this freewheeling, exhilarating, excited quality, such as spinning round and round until dizziness takes over or rolling hysterically down a grassy bank. Entering a dark shed, closing the door and screaming in mock terror might be another example of when children deliberately inflict this 'voluptuous panic' on themselves, momentarily destroying the stability of perception 'upping the ante' in exaggerating the mock terror. This is very different from the body tension and cautious trepidation that might characterize real fear of dark places. Such play, Caillois argues, produces intoxicating pleasure and plays a strong part in friendship, group camaraderie and social cohesion. Caillois identified fairground rides, skiing and racing cars as adult forms of dizzy play. Today, we could add bungee jumping, sky diving, zip wire riding and many more. Yet much of the opportunity for 'dizzy play' for children has been replaced by adult managed theme park rides such as roller coasters or adrenaline busting rides, such as 'Oblivion' or 'Nemesis'. These provide the sensation of falling, spinning or whirling with accompanying shrieking, the 'voluptuous panic' but without any real world risk of danger.

However, there is a very real difference between these forms of entertainment and children's play. There is no skill required to ride the roller coaster. Someone else is in control. Of course, you need some degree of bravado and daring to attempt it, but the risks are virtually non-existent. Risk taking in play, however, allows you to demonstrate your competence; it requires instant judgements about danger and about safety, and some planning and foresight. Ultimately, you are in control and your safety depends on what you do. Mistakes may be as amusing as success—the toboggan tips over in a pile of snow and everyone laughs—but they provide immediate feedback and allow for variation and refinement of technique. If all our thrills are of the roller coaster type then we relinquish this control, and rely only on the risk assessments and safety records of others.

What is risky play?

Stephenson researched the concept of risky physical play in New Zealand kindergartens. She was fascinated by the prevalence of children's use of the word 'scary' and their deliberate attempts to search out scary situations. She identified three significant elements which made an experience seem 'risky' to a four-year-old.

* attempting something never done before;
* feeling on the borderlines of 'out of control' often because of height or speed;
* overcoming fear (Stephenson 2003: 36).

She noted that slides and swings could be scary as they combined both height and speed. Often children would increase the risk or scariness by setting themselves additional challenges, for example, using a polystyrene board to increase the speed of descent on a slide or fixing a portable tunnel on the slide to increase the challenge of sliding through it.

Attempting something when the outcome is uncertain is also a feature of risk requiring a certain amount of 'daring'. Such things as balancing across a wobbly bridge or, on a much smaller scale, holding a cold and wet snail in the palm of your hand or reaching out to stroke a rabbit, are very risky when the outcome is uncertain. In the same

Figure 6.1 Children often increase the risk or 'scariness' by setting themselves additional challenges.

way other aspects of play can be considered 'risky', for example, risking the collapse of a construction by adding another brick, playing rough and tumble where the risk of your actions being 'read' in the wrong way by another child could be high, transgressing rules or roles by engaging in nonsense. Teasing and jokes are also risky because the outcome is unknown. From this perspective most imaginative play involves an element of risk in the sense that a characteristic of play is that it is uncertain and unpredictable, and therefore risky requiring high levels of negotiation.

What do we mean by risk?

Little (2006) defines a risk as any behaviour in which there is uncertainty about the outcomes. It involves a consideration of the benefits against the possible undesirable consequences of the behaviour, as well as the probability of success or failure.

Lindon (1999) distinguishes between a risk and a hazard. She argues that a hazard is a physical situation that could potentially offer harm. A risk is the probability that this hazard will be realized and that someone will be harmed as a result. However, notions of risk have changed over the centuries with many commentators suggesting that the word risk was first used in the Middle Ages to refer to the possibilities of disasters and perils that could befall sea voyages (Lupton 1999). This perspective viewed risk as an 'act of God', outside all human control. Later risk became a mathematical formula of probability in gambling to help predict potential losses and gains from certain moves in card games. It was an attempt to bring some scientific calculation and, therefore, an element of certainty to a game of chance. Having some awareness of probability allows us to weigh up the risk as against the benefit.

However, current notions of risk have little to do with probabilities and, as Douglas (1992: 24) argues, risk to most people now means danger. High risk means high danger. Parents are unlikely to be swayed by the evidence that the probability of a child being harmed by a stranger is extremely low and has hardly changed in the last decade. The perception and fear of 'stranger danger' is so powerful that statistics and probabilities have little meaning. It is, as Jackson and Scott argue, the pessimistic version of doing the lottery—'It might be me' (Jackson and Scott 1999: 93). While there is any chance that 'it might be me', it is easier to reduce the uncertainty by eliminating the risk. Beck (1993) argues that we have become a risk society plagued by risk anxiety and Furedi (2002) that we live in a culture of fear. As we saw in Chapter 1 the effect of this climate of fear is to reduce children's autonomy so that they generally have few opportunities to play unsupervised or out of sight of adults.

However, the concept of risk is clearly problematic. Risks are not absolutes, there is no such thing as a risk in reality, only perceptions of risk. Risk is socially constructed, and what is acceptable in one context or in one culture may be unacceptable in another. What is an acceptable risk for one child may be a hazard to another. Gender plays a significant part and research suggests that parents perceive risk taking to be more acceptable for boys than it is for girls (Morrongiello and Hogg 2004). Risk then is embedded with values about what is considered appropriate or inappropriate for children. I often use photographs as prompts for discussion in seminar sessions with students. Photographs of children climbing high, sliding down a steep slide or making a fire, promote fierce debate as to whether these experiences might be acceptable in a nursery setting. A student from Ghana recollects her experience, aged three, of being trusted to help cook on an open fire. A student from the UK finds it totally unacceptable to consider having a fire in her own setting. Others disagree and give examples of well-managed use of fires for cooking outdoors. Such exchanges challenge our expectations of what young children, in a supportive social context, are able to do and to manage.

Safe as possible or safe as necessary?

It is not just the word 'risk', which is problematic; the notion of safety is problematic too. Most early childhood settings mention safety in their statement of aims. A typical phrase might be 'we aim to provide a safe and secure environment for children to develop and learn'. Yet the word safe means different things to different people, and is dependent on values and perceptions of children and childhood. What is a safe and secure environment? Is it one where children are protected from every possible source of harm and thereby kept dependent, metaphorically wrapped in cotton wool? It could be argued that such an environment cannot be safe because it fails to offer challenge and thereby denies children the opportunities to develop the skills to be safe, and creates another even greater potential risk, a generation of children who are either timid or reckless.

The danger of creating supposedly risk-free environments is that adults' expectations can remain low as children do not have the chance to demonstrate their competence. A culture of low expectations and risk aversion can lead to dull, unstimulating environments where the adults' focus is on containing and managing those children who are often, literally and metaphorically, climbing up the wall searching for excitement and challenge.

If environments can be too safe then safety cannot be an ultimate objective. A safe environment, I would argue, is one where safety is not seen as safety *from* all possible harm, but offers safety *to* explore, experiment, try things out and to take risks. Such an environment should never make claims to be safe because accidents are always possible, but should promote awareness of and management of risk as part of its ethos. It should as the title of a conference of the Royal Society of Prevention of Accidents (RoSPA) stated be 'as safe as necessary not as safe as possible'.

As there is a growing challenge to our health- and safety-obsessed culture, and increasing emphasis on the importance of risk and challenge in children's outdoor play areas has the balance swung too far? Judith and John Hicks argue that, far from being the negative phenomena that it is generally considered to be, children's health and safety legislation is largely a good thing. They argue that 'it seems currently fashionable in Britain to underplay the potentially lethal or crippling aspects of risk in relation to children's play space' (Hicks and Hicks 2005: 10). They take exception to a position paper on risk produced by the Play Safety Forum, particularly the following statement: 'Exposure to real risk in playgrounds provides beneficial learning experiences and a sought after thrill' (Play Safety Forum 2002: 3). They argue that such a statement is indicative of a growing trend to downplay or even to tolerate known risks of injury in children's play areas. They provocatively suggest that 'one might speculate on measures such as delaying the repair of damaged guard rails . . . removing restrictions on dog fouling in play space . . .' and so on (Hicks and Hicks 2005: 211).

The examples used are unhelpful as damaged equipment or dog fouled spaces do not add any value to play, and can clearly detract from play by creating damaged or soiled environments. However, a serious point does emerge in this apparent conflict of ideas. There is a real danger that the expertise of those like the Hicks', who have studied play equipment design and playground safety for decades, is lost in a move to encouraging risky play outdoors. There seems to be no doubt at all that potential hazards such as gaps in play equipment, which could allow for heads or limbs to become trapped, should be eliminated. A splintered wooden slide is clearly dangerous for a young child who would not expect or anticipate such a hazard in a piece of equipment. Observations of children's use of equipment and analyses of accidents over many years are clearly important to our understanding of risk and safety outdoors. There is a huge gap between those who are interested in and study the benefits of play, and those who are interested in and study play as a source of injury for children. We need to open up a dialogue so that we can all become more expert in our understanding of the benefits and risks of play.

An environment that is as safe as necessary seeks to remove hazards that offer no play value, but actively promotes risk and risk awareness, and accepts that accidents are an intrinsic part of children's play and that risk taking is part of the value of play.

Why risky play?

The problem with the risk discourse is that it has focused on risk as a negative concept with little emphasis on the benefits of risk in play. Risks can be calculated and accident rates measured, but the benefits of play are less easily quantified. Young children's play and the value of risk taking is not always recognized or well understood. However, if a case for risky, challenging play is to be made, then it is essential that we are able to justify it. Evidence would suggest that risk taking is linked with key areas of children's learning.

First, risk taking is part of life. Being able to assess and manage risk is a life skill that we need for survival. As adults we weigh up the risks and benefits of particular activities, and make decisions as to what to do. If we choose to go skiing we know the risk of returning from holiday with a broken bone, but may decide the pleasure of skiing, the exhilaration, the contributions to health and well being are worth that potential risk. Indeed, the riskiness of the activity might be central to its attraction.

Bumps, bruises, tumbles and falls are part of learning as children learn to crawl, stand, run, ride bikes and learn about their bodies in relation to the world. Assessing and managing risk is a skill that needs to be developed, practised and refined if we are not to succumb to overwhelming anxiety or to recklessness. As Moss and Petrie argue:

> Risk is inherent in human endeavour, and for children not to engage with it is for them to be cut off from an important part of life . . . People learn to assess and manage risk by encountering it coming to understand the balance to be achieved between the positive and negative outcomes of their actions.
>
> (Moss and Petrie 2002: 130)

Secondly, there are positive associations between risk taking and children's well being and learning. Taking risks allow children to learn at the very edge of their capabilities, it pushes out boundaries, extends limits and enhances opportunities (see Figure 6.2). Vygotsky (1978)

Figure 6.2 Taking risks allows children to learn at the very edge of their capabilities, pushes their boundaries, extends limits and enhances opportunities.

argued that we should focus our attention on what children can nearly do, that is the 'buds' or emerging skills and understanding, rather than the fruits of development. He argued that what children can do with some encouragement and help from others they will soon be able to do on their own. Risk taking allows children to push themselves further and to extend their limits. Risk taking in play allows children to vary the familiar, to try out new ideas. For example as soon as children have gained competence at riding a bike, then they start to try increasingly difficult manoeuvres leading to such things as stunt riding involving leaps into the air. With adult support and encouragement new skills can be learnt and new achievements gained. Children with disabilities, especially, are entitled to encounter risk and challenge:

> All children both need and want to take risks in order to explore limits, venture into new experiences and develop their capacities ... Children with disabilities have an equal if not greater need for opportunities to take risks, since they may be denied the freedom of choice enjoyed by their non-disabled peers.
>
> (Play Safety Forum 2002)

Thirdly, research by Carole Dweck suggests that a sense of 'mastery', an 'I can do it' attitude, a willingness to try things out and to take risks are important characteristics of effective learners. She contrasts what she terms 'mastery' children who have a strong sense of self-efficacy and who see challenges to be relished, rather than avoided with those she terms 'helpless' who tend to lack persistence, give up easily with an 'I can't do it' attitude. Her research suggests that positive dispositions of mastery are key to successful learning (Dweck 2000: 7).

Most interesting of all, she found that these dispositions were not just personality traits, but were developed or inhibited by the environment and the attitudes of those around them. Clearly, an environment where children are discouraged from taking risks, where adults themselves are anxious and fearful are less likely to develop the disposition to persist, to see challenges as problems to enjoy, rather than things to fear.

> It doesn't help a child to tackle a difficult task if they succeed constantly on an easy one. It doesn't teach them to persist in the face of obstacles if obstacles are always eliminated.
>
> (Dweck, cited in Claxton 1999: 35)

Claxton argues that risk taking is part of the 'toolkit' of effective learners and that developing young children's resilience and willingness to take risks may be important for children's persistence in the face of challenge (Claxton 1999).

Finally, risk taking in play appears to be positively associated with emotional well being, resilience and mental health. A study by the UK Mental Health Foundation argued that the lack of risk in play was damaging children's well being and resilience, and leading to

Figure 6.3 Taking risks develops positive dispositions and an 'I can do it' attitude.

increased numbers of children with mental health problems requiring professional help. 'Unsupervised play enables children to take risks, to think through decisions, and gain increased self-confidence and greater resilience' the report stated. (Mental Health Foundation 1999: 36). Playing outside develops interdependence, rather than dependence on adults, as children have to look out for each other, anticipate and manage unpredictable situations. Managing fear and uncertainty and holding your nerve when feeling on the borderline of out of control, one of the elements of 'scary' identified by Stephenson (2003), could be considered vitally important in emotional well being (Figure 6.3).

However, it is wrong to assume that risk taking is all positive. Clearly, young children can take risks that are not appropriate, which border on recklessness and put themselves or others at risk of harm. I watched a four-year-old struggle to lift a pram up the steps of a slide, and then attempt to put a younger child into the pram with the intention of pushing both down the slide. Clearly, this was a potential hazard, however innovative the idea. In this example, the adult intervened, but allowed the child to push the empty pram and to watch as it tumbled over the edge of the slide and crashed to the ground. The experience offered scope for some sober reflection and discussion on what if . . .? Children need to learn how to assess risks themselves, but they lack experience, and sometimes need the help of more experienced children and adults. In this we way we 'loan' them our experience and foresight in order to help them to begin to assess risk for themselves. Clearly, strategies of wariness and caution are part of being a good risk taker, and children learn these from their own first-hand experience, but also from working alongside adults, for example, learning how to use tools safely.

Risk taking is not just about taking physical risks. Children take social risks when they try to join an established game. The risk of rejection is high and strategies are needed to access the play. A toddler takes an emotional risk when he moves away from a trusted adult to venture in new and unexplored territory. Children are not necessarily competent in all areas and a competent physical risk taker is not necessarily a competent social risk taker. However, the confidence generated from one area of risk taking is likely to impact on other aspects of development. While there is little firm evidence to suggest a causal relationship, we can postulate that there may be some connection between physical risk taking and a willingness to take risks in other aspects of learning. Creativity, for example, requires the ability to take some risks, a willingness to go beyond the accepted, the routine, the given. Claxton argues that to be creative you have to 'dare to be different' (Claxton, cited in Moyles 1989: 80). Scientific hypothesizing also requires conjecturing, a willingness to take an imaginative leap, to be excited by the unexpected, to live 'on the edge', rather than accepting the given.

Is outdoor play dangerous?

Fear of serious accident in play outdoors is not supported by evidence. Across the UK there is one fatality on a school or public playground every three or four years. While any fatality is tragic, it has to be seen in the context of between five- and six-hundred children who die from accidents in the home and on the streets in any year. In fact, deaths from playground accidents are so rare that it is difficult to identify any causal pattern, although an analysis suggests that most are unrelated to children's play or to play equipment. The majority of playground accidents result in little more than cuts, abrasions and bruising, and make up only 2 per cent of all accident and emergency admissions in the UK. Children are many times more likely to be hurt in a traffic accident or in an accident in the home than in outdoor play (Ball: 2002).

This is not to suggest that we become complacent about accidents outdoors, but that we become more literate in our understanding of risk and the likely causes of accidents. For example, there has been no noticeable decline in playground fatalities in the last decade, despite the high profile media campaigns and heavy investment in safety surfacing. There is also some evidence of an increase in upper limb fractures, possibly caused by the false sense of security or 'lulling effect' that safety surfacing can engender, leading to children recklessly jumping from heights expecting the safety surface to cushion their fall (Ball 2002). Playground accidents are also very modest compared with sports injuries from games like football, rugby, hockey and cricket. Because such games have a higher status than play, injuries are deemed to be inevitable and more socially acceptable.

After reviewing all the evidence in a report for the UK Health and Safety Executive, Ball concluded that:

> In comparison with other activities and locations playgrounds in the UK are not as sometimes implied a hot bed of danger. This raises the question of why playground safety has been such a prominent issue. It seems plausible that the answer is that this particular risk has been culturally selected, that is chosen on the basis of factors associated more with the workings of society than with critical analysis.
>
> (Ball 2002: 61)

Trusting children

While risk anxiety might be a pervasive feature of modern society, concern about children's safety was clearly an issue in the nineteenth century and Froebel discusses a parent's concern at a child climbing high up a tree.

> If we could remember our joy when in childhood we looked out beyond the cramping limits of our immediate surroundings we should not be so insensitive as to call out 'come down you will fall'. One learns to protect oneself from falling by looking over and around a place as well as by physical movement and the ordinary thing certainly looks quite different from above. Ought we not then to give the boy opportunities for an enlargement of his view which will broaden his thoughts and feelings?
>
> 'But he will be reckless and I shall never be free of anxiety about him'.
>
> No, the boy whose training has always been connected with the gradual development of his capacities will attempt only a little more than he has already been able to do, and will come safely through all these dangers. It is the boy who does not

know his strength and the demands made on it who is likely to venture beyond his experience and run into unsuspected danger.

(Froebel, in Lilley 1967: 126)

What is interesting about this exchange is that Froebel focuses not on the risk, but on the benefits of tree climbing to a child's learning. He identifies the sense of joy and freedom associated with being high up, the opportunities for learning about height and perspective, the broadening of a child's thoughts, as well as feelings about the world, and the building up of experience that will contribute to the child's safety in the future. He argues that, with experience, children recognize their own limits, and that with trusting adults they act safely and not recklessly. He sees children as competent, rather than incompetent.

Froebel was part of the romantic movement and it is interesting that the romantic view of childhood as free, innocent, natural, where children were encouraged to roam over hills through fields, woods and forests, to climb cliffs and explore caves, included a view of childhood where exposure to potential risk and danger was seen as part of life, not something children should be shielded from. Freedom in play involved the opportunity to do things, not protection from things. It involved trusting children. Trusting children requires knowledge of their capabilities, their confidence and a willingness to relinquish some control. Trusting children communicates respect for children's intentions and a willingness to share responsibility. Trusting children, for example, to use a hose pipe to fill up the water tray or paddling pool, to carry equipment safely, to use real tools (Figure 6.4) to help light a fire allows children to develop the necessary confidence, competence and 'know how' to be safe.

Stinging nettles?

A coordinator of the Redford House Nursery at Froebel College, Roehampton University kept a patch of nettles in the outdoor area arguing that nettles and stings were things that urban children should learn about. Is this appropriate provision for young children? I posed this question to a group of undergraduates, but little anticipated the vehemence of the debate that followed! Views polarized around whether it was uncaring to allow children to be hurt and possibly distressed, or whether it was uncaring not to help children experience something that was part of life. While there is no simple right or wrong answer, in this case it does raise questions about our view of

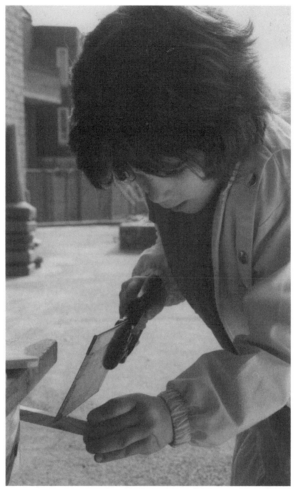

Figure 6.4 Trusting children to use real tools and teaching the skills to use them safely has been a long-standing part of the nursery tradition.

childhood. Should early childhood settings be places where every source of possible hurt is removed and where children are kept happy at all costs, or do we see childhood as a time of learning through experience where risks are part of life and, therefore, should also be part of our nursery settings? Too much emphasis on happiness can lead to over protective environments, where the normal trips and tumbles, bumps and bruises of childhood are screened out, and where children do not experience the joy of taking risks.

I would argue that an essential part of the survival toolkit that children need to learn at a young age is knowledge that some plants are dangerous to touch and others are dangerous to eat, and that some caution and adult guidance is necessary before identifying those plants with which they can safely play. A patch of stinging nettles would seem to be entirely acceptable in enabling discussion on this, as well as offering some learning through first-hand experience. Poisonous plants, on the other hand, could be considered an unacceptable hazard in a play environment, but should be seen and talked about on visits outside the setting.

What does this mean in practice?

While it is easy to blame others, policy makers, planners, parents, health and safety officers, the key to developing more opportunities for risky play lies with those who work with young children. Stephenson (2003) argued that the children's hunger for physical challenge was satisfied more through the practitioners' attitudes than the provision itself. For example, adults who enjoyed being outside, who were interested in physical play, and took a sensitive and liberal approach to supervision, enabled children to find challenges that were experienced as risky, but did not put them in a position of hazard.

This requires confidence, sensitivity, knowledge of young children's play, knowledge of individual children, but it also requires a framework of support to help adults develop the confidence to open up possibilities for risk and challenge. Research on practitioners' perspectives on risk suggests that practitioners reveal considerable 'risk anxiety', and fear of accident, culpability and possible litigation when working with children in outdoor environments (Tovey 2006). In some settings, preventing children from taking risks can be one way of managing this anxiety. However, in other settings, risky play is publicly celebrated, for example, through displays of photographs and captions, through supportive policies and close relationships with parents. One practitioner said 'We have a big poster which says "Risky play is encouraged here". We want children to feel safe to take risks . . . We tell them [parents] we can't guarantee accidents won't happen' (Tovey 2006).

Recent legal judgements offer some evidence that attitudes may be changing. Take this quote from Lord Scott (Tomlinson v Congleton Borough Council 2004), for example. 'Of course there is some risk of accidents arising from the joie de vivre of the young. But that is no reason for imposing a grey and dull safety regime on everyone' (cited

in Spiegal 2007). The Play Safety Forum has produced a policy statement that is unambiguous in its support for acceptable levels of risk in
play provision. It is approved by both lawyers and the Health and
Safety Executive and could provide a useful framework for developing
a policy on risk and safety in early years settings (Play Safety Forum
2002).

Some implications for practice

First, there is an urgent need for the issues of risk and play to be
debated within nursery teams. Without shared understanding about
risky play outdoors and without a shared sense of trust within the
team, staff can be left anxious and unsupported. 'If a staff team will
not take risks together, to debate difficult issues or to be innovative,
allowing children to take risks will be much more difficult' (P. Elfer
2006, personal communication). There is also a need for a debate with
parents and the wider community, including landscape architects,
planners, and health and safety officers.

Secondly, assessing and managing risk is complex and multi-
layered. It requires considerable knowledge of the nature of young
children's play, as well as of individual children's competencies.
Where do early childhood practitioners and play providers learn
these skills? If we want a generation of confident children willing to
embrace risk and challenge, then we need to develop confident adults
who have a deeper understanding of the issues surrounding risk and
play, which goes well beyond a narrow 'health and safety' agenda.
This has important implications for training.

Thirdly, accepting that risk is an essential characteristic of both
play and pedagogy requires adults to engage more closely with children's intentions so that play can be extended, rather than curtailed.
This can have positive benefits for all aspects of children's play.
Developing a language of risk and safety can help children to
become more literate in their understanding of risk and in developing
safe ways of doing things. This is explored further in Chapter 8 of
this book.

Finally, if we deny children the opportunities to be risk takers we
may risk creating a generation of children who may be either reckless
in their pursuit of thrills and excitement or risk averse, lacking the
confidence and skill to be safe, but also lacking the disposition to take
metaphoric leaps in the dark, and to be innovative and creative in
their thinking. As Claxton argues 'reckless exploration jeopardises
survival but so does a persistent refusal to engage with the unknown'
(Claxton 1999: 41):

And then the day came when
the risk to remain tight in a bud was more painful
than the risk it took to blossom.

(Anais Nin)

7

WHAT DO WE MEAN BY FREE PLAY OUTDOORS?

Play is a difficult concept, and by its very nature cannot be pinned down or precisely defined. There is nothing tangible, predictable or certain about children's play, and this makes thinking about play more difficult and sometimes uncomfortable for those who like things neat and orderly. Play sits uneasily in a culture of standards, measurable outcomes, testing, targets and quality control.

The notion of 'free play' so valued by the pioneers of early childhood education was widely criticized in the 1980s by researchers such as Sylva *et al* (1980) and Hutt *et al* (1989). They found that, far from being challenging, much play was low level, mundane, fleeting and repetitive. Although aspects of the methodology and the theoretical perspectives underpinning the research are open to question, it was not difficult to find settings where play outdoors resembled these findings.

The research contributed to a demand to impose more structure on play. The introduction of the Desirable Learning Outcomes (School Curriculum and Assessment Authority 1996) and then the Early Learning Goals and the Curriculum Guidance for the Foundation Stage (QCA 2000) attempted to identify more precisely the learning outcomes of play and to spell out what, specifically, children might learn through play. It could be argued that there is little wrong with this, after all if we make the claim that children learn as they play then we need to be able to identify and communicate to others what that learning might be.

However, the language of play has changed. Rather than referring to play or to free play many writers refer, rather defensively to 'structured play' or 'purposeful play', to 'well planned play' or even to 'directed play'. It is rare to find reference to the notion of 'free play' in any official documents, although the term 'free flow play' (Bruce 1991) is used by many practitioners. This has shifted attention away from what children do in play to what adults do. The change in language about play has been accompanied, I would argue, with a lack of confidence in play so that early years practitioners increasingly seek to justify play by reference to curriculum objectives. For example, the carefully planned play shop set up outdoors is justified by reference to mathematics, including shapes, sorting, matching, counting and money. It seems that the more uncertain we are about play, the more we attempt to translate it into some clearly recognized learning outcome. In practice, the children may very well learn about mathematics, but the likelihood is that they will remove the food, put it in bags or trolleys, transport it around the play area, open the carefully prepared packages, argue about who is the shopkeeper and totally transform the play into one of burglars, shoplifters, guard dogs and policemen. As Dunn observed shopping play for young children is much more exciting and 'anarchic' than the replaying of conventional events in reality and is just as likely to turn into a Cinderella story or even end up with the players going to the moon (Dunn 2004: 26). This can leave adults despairing about play and urging children to 'play nicely'. However, play is messy and unpredictable, it flows from one theme to another and its outcome is uncertain. It seems that the more play is pre-planned and pre-packaged, the more adults and children are set up for disappointment as their agendas diverge.

Uncertainty about the value of play itself and lack of shared understanding about the terms used to discuss play has contributed to some collective confusion about play. Siraj-Blatchford *et al* (2006: 85) made much the same point in an interim evaluation report on the implementation of the Foundation Phase in Wales suggesting that the use of terminology such as play, free play, and structured play caused confusion and recommending further clarification. So what do these notions of play mean?

Structured play

The term 'structured play' suggests that play is somehow more rigorous, more likely to lead to desirable learning if it is pre-structured by adults. However, all outdoor play is structured in some way. It is structured by the physical and cultural context of the setting, the values, whether implicit or explicit, of those who work there, how time and space are organized and the resources that are provided. As McAuley and Jackson (1992) have argued these hidden structures are very powerful in shaping what goes on.

Both Sylva and Bruner argued, in the 1980s, that structure is a characteristic of materials and activities themselves. Structured materials and activities such as construction materials, art activities and jigsaw puzzles, they argued, are the most challenging and unstructured materials, such as sand and water, and open-ended resources outdoors lack any clear goal structure and, therefore, do not challenge children's minds (Bruner 1980; Sylva *et al* 1980).

However, Athey offers a very different perspective on structure. For her, structure is not in the material, but in the thinking that each child brings to it. 'External objects do not have cognitive structure; cognitive structure is a feature of mind' (Athey 1990: 33). Structure, she argues, refers to the underpinning structures of children's thought evident through their patterns of repeatable behaviours or schemas. By identifying these structures of thought or 'patterns of persistent concern' (Athey 1990: 363) adults can enrich them with worthwhile curriculum content. For example, children showing a strong rotational schema might be taken to visit a windmill and provided with resources such as water wheels to explore in the garden.

Gussin Paley also suggests, from a very different perspective, that structure is inherent in children's play. She argues that children bring to their play a powerful socially constructed way of organizing and thinking about experience—the story structure:

> How can the least structured activity . . . promise the greatest practice in concentration on a subject? The answer of course is that fantasy play is not the least structured activity, though the structure is not provided by the teacher. The children are using the most reliable structure for thinking about anything—story.
> (Gussin Paley 1990: 92)

Both Gussin Paley and Athey see play as already structured by children. What are required are informed adults who can notice, observe and tune in to the underpinning structures of the play and extend them in ways that are rigorous and worthwhile.

Given that play is already structured is there any need for adults to 'pre-structure' it? The involvement of an adult can lead to play that is more complex, sustained and intellectually rigorous than many pre-structured activities (Sestini 1987). The REPEY project has confirmed that free play supported by sensitive adult interaction can be a particularly rich context for learning (Siraj-Blatchford *et al* 2002). Structure, it seems, can be **in** an activity or imposed **on** play before it begins, or it can be developed **through** the play constructed by the particpants (adapted from Sestini 1987: 29). It is the latter, Sestini argued, that leads to richer and more challenging play.

Resources that are thoughtfully selected and prepared, which provoke interest and ideas, or suggest links and connections, and which are roughly tuned to children's prevailing interests, concerns and existing understanding along with sensitive adults who make time to understanding and develop the themes of the play can provide a rich context for play to flourish.

Directed play

Play ... directed? There would appear to be a contradiction here. Generally accepted characteristics of play are that it is freely chosen and intrinsically motivated (Garvey 1991: 4; Bruce 2004: 149). Play can, at times, be initiated by adults, but to proceed there has to be a sense of engagement and shared involvement. The term directed play suggests that the adult retains control over the course and direction of the activity so that it no longer meets the criteria of play. Huizinga, in his classic text *Homo Ludens*, argued that 'all play is a voluntary activity. Play to order is no longer play; it [can] at best be a forcible imitation of it (Huizinga 1950: 7).

Nevertheless, the term directed play features in early childhood literature. Moyles, for example, argues that bouts of free play should alternate with bouts of directed play, which can then enrich the subsequent free play (Moyles 1989: 16). The danger of this model is that the subsequent free play becomes increasingly modelled on the adults' ideas, rather than having an energy and impetus of its own. Adults can teach skills, give relevant information, extend children's thinking, but this is very different from directing children's play.

Studies of young children's play reveal the often competent and complex ways that children direct and negotiate their own play, smoothly shifting between roles of director, actor and narrator within the same play episode (for example, Garvey 1991). Children develop skill in planning, negotiating and compromising as they agree the characters, script and plot, and determine the course and direction of the play. Often play is suspended while this negotiation takes place (Trawick-Smith 1998b). Play that is directed or dominated by adults undermines these important developing competencies.

Controlled play

Issues concerning play and the words we use to talk about it are made more complex by the evidence that what practitioners say about play is not always what they do. For example Polakow (1992), drawing on observations of day care settings in America, identified what she termed 'controlled play'. Although a session might be labelled 'free play', in practice the play was controlled and directed by adults who were over anxious that children should be both busy and safe, and therefore kept 'hovering over' and interfering in their play.

> I began to interpret this safety concern as an anxious reaction on the part of the staff, an attempt to monitor that which was free-flowing and unstructured. To impose a manifest structure on 'free play' would be too blatant an educational contradiction, but a latent structure masked by the legitimate concern for safety effectively converted 'free play' into 'controlled play' in a manner that was socially acceptable to the staff.
>
> (Polakow 1992: 64)

Such 'latent structures' can be hidden from view, but are powerfully influential in shaping children's play. The point that Polakow is making here is also a reminder that other research studies, which purport to focus on and draw conclusion about free play, are possibly not studying free play at all, but something else entirely.

Well planned play

The phrase 'well planned play' was used in the UK Curriculum Guidance for the Foundation Stage. For example, the document stated that 'well planned play is a key way in which children learn with enjoyment and challenge' (QCA 2000: 7). This suggested that play that is not just planned, but **well** planned is qualitatively different from play that is 'free', somehow implying that it is more rigorous and challenging.

It implied that the planning is done by the adults, but what does well planned play really mean? Clearly, there are many aspects of the outdoor environment that require careful planning, resources, first-hand experiences, space and time, for example. Strategies for adult engagement and interaction also need to be planned, but the essence of play is its spontaneity and its unpredictability, which cannot be pre-planned by adults. Children initiate, plan and negotiate their own play, and much time is taken up with this planning before the enactment begins. Adults clearly have an important role in helping children to plan and negotiate play. Trawick-Smith (1998b), for example, suggests that adults model appropriate negotiating and planning strategies as part of play. However, I suspect that this is not what is implied by the term well planned play. The danger of play that is 'well planned' is that the course and direction of the play has been decided by the adults. If adults have planned an activity with clearly identified learning outcomes then 'success' is predicated on achievement of those outcomes and the focus of the adult's attention is more likely to be geared towards those ends often at the expense of more interesting diversions.

With the introduction of the new Early Years Foundation Stage the language about play has changed again. The Practice Guidance places more emphasis on 'spontaneous play' and indicates that practitioners 'provide *well planned experiences* based on children's *spontaneous play*' (Department for Education and Skills 2007: 7, my emphasis). Practitioners are urged to observe and reflect on children's spontaneous play and build on this by planning and resourcing a challenging environment. This is a subtle shift in emphasis closer to the notion of 'free play'.

Free play

Isaacs argued that 'play has the greatest value for the child when it is really free and his own' (Isaacs 1929: 133). Yet the notion of free play was criticized in the 1980s and, far from being challenging, was found to be often desultory, fleeting and 'low level'. Researchers such as Sylva *et al* (1980) and Hutt *et al* (1989) suggested that play lacked structure and, in particular, it lacked sustained adult involvement. Outdoor play was seen as offering 'total expression', which teachers were advised to 'cut down on'. From my experience, it was not difficult to find settings at that time where play had low status and where adults took such a 'hands off', *laissez faire* approach. Outdoor play in particular was (and still can be) confused with recreation with children left to their own devices 'free' from adult interference.

However, is this what free play means? Certainly, it bears little resemblance to the notion of free play that Isaacs and Froebel promoted. Some of the confusion comes from the use of the word 'free'. Often the term is interpreted as meaning *free from* any restrictions or adult involvement or influence. However, freedom is not about unrestrained '*laissez faire*' or licence to do as you please. Freedom is about opportunity to do things not just the removal of barriers. As philosophers such as Isaiah Berlin have discussed, there is also a positive notion of freedom, *freedom to* which is concerned with mastery, self-control and self-determination (Berlin 1969: 144). Froebel also argued that the child is:

free to determine his own actions according to the laws and

demands of the play he is involved in, and through and in his play he is able to feel himself to be independent and autonomous.

(Froebel, cited in Leibschner 1992)

Play to Froebel involved a 'constant interaction between law, freedom and life' (Leibschner 1992: 60) indicating that freedom and discipline were not separate. Vygotsky (1978) also identified the paradoxical nature of play, that children are free from 'situational constraints', but at the same time are subject to the rules of the play.

Freedom is not just about removing restrictions because other factors intervene to limit children's choices and opportunities. Rather it is a question of identifying what particular liberties and what particular restraints are most likely to promote those values, which we consider to be most important. Freedom is about opportunity for action not merely action itself. It is about what paths are open and what closed, and about opportunities to forge new ones. It is freedom to do 'what' that matters for freedom is not a neutral term, it takes on the values of those who use it. To be free to do something requires opportunity, encouragement and some recognition of its value. It also requires restrictions on other factors that might limit that opportunity. Outdoor play which is relegated to something which is done after the completion of 'work' or takes place in a dull and unstimulating environment or which is constantly interrupted by set routines, and which denies children control over their own play themes, is not 'free' because paths have already been closed and potential restricted. Similarly, play that is not valued by adults, and has no adult support or extension is not 'free' because its potential is constrained.

Bruce (1991, 2004) promotes the concept of rich, sustained play or what she terms 'free flow play', which is characterized by a state of 'flow' that is intense, sustained over time, and involves deep concentration and involvement. Such play requires time, space, resources and adult support, but not adult domination if it is to develop.

Knowledge of what promotes and restricts opportunities for rich play and learning outdoors allows us to take more responsibility, to intervene more actively and to reflect more critically on adults' roles in enriching play, for example, the way time and space are structured, the provision that is made and how adults interact with children's play.

The findings of the REPEY research on settings deemed to be good or excellent, has confirmed that free play supported by sensitive adult interaction can be a rich context for learning (Siraj Blatchford *et al* 2002). Less widely publicized is the finding that a majority of

Figure 7.1 In free play children create their own challenges. This child was totally involved in digging channels and building bridges.

observations deemed to be 'high challenge' did not include adults at all, suggesting that adult interaction is not an essential requirement for rich and challenging play, but that possibly quality interaction in some episodes continues to enrich what children do when they play on their own.

Confusions can also arise over the use of the word 'play'. Research on practitioners' perspectives on the word play suggests that most define play as 'freely chosen activity' in contrast to a directed task. However, not all freely chosen activity is necessarily play and Bruce (1991) draws a distinction between play and what she refers to as first-hand experience. She argues that much of what children do in their everyday life is not play, but is first-hand experience. Outdoor activities such as gardening, building a pond, making and cooking on a fire, cleaning out the rabbit's cage, filling up the sand pit are not play, they are real world experiences. They may, at times, move into play, for example, when children cleaning the rabbit's cage pretend to be rabbits and hop around the garden, but they remain different from play. Play uses first-hand experience and imagination, and re-shapes them. I would argue that adult planning, structuring and sometimes directing children's first-hand experience outdoors is essential. Young children have very little experience of the world and much of the task of the adult is to build on children's interests and concerns, and broaden their experience. Building a pond, planting a vegetable garden, making a fountain, organizing trips out all require careful planning and consideration so that the purpose and intentions are clear. This, I would suggest, is very different from the planning, structuring and directing of play.

Given that play in early childhood settings is not 'free', but operates within many different structures, I would suggest that the notion of free play as a positive principle of enablement offers more to young children than the notions of structured, directed or well planned play, which suggest that the course of the play is already determined by adults. Free play outdoors in an environment that is well planned to promote risk taking, provoke curiosity, foster relationships, support creativity and cultivate imagination offers more scope for challenging play than the pre-packaged, pre-planned activities that are often called 'play', but are a poor substitute for rich play.

> Children's right to play in and out of school must be upheld not simply as a means to facilitate development and learning but because the freedom it entails is essential for the child and for society.
>
> (Brehony 2004: 37)

8

ROLES, RESOURCES AND RELATIONSHIPS OUTDOORS

> Making the environment beautiful and challenging is not an end in itself: it is a means to an end. And the end is more important than the means. So it is what children [and adults] *do* when they play out of doors that is the heart of the matter.
>
> (Drummond 1995: 3)

When an environment is rich and challenging, it is all too easy to assume that the children's play will be equally so, but this is not always the case. I have seen mundane play in the most aesthetically beautiful environments and rich, sustained play in environments that appear unpromising, but with sensitive adult support can provide scope for creative and innovative play. This is not an argument for impoverished environments, but an argument for the role of the adult. The key is how adults and children adapt to each other in transforming spaces and in sustaining play.

> Children who spend all their time in the open air may still observe nothing of its beauties. The boy sees the significance but if he does not find the same awareness in adults the seed of knowledge just beginning to germinate is crushed.
>
> (Froebel, cited in Lilley 1967: 146)

Research, although very limited, has been mostly critical of adults' roles in children's play outdoors. Hutt *et al*, for example, noted that there can be 'an implicit agreement between staff and children about what one does outdoors as opposed to the indoor situation' (1989: 81). They found that the adult role changed from being mainly interactive indoors to being predominantly monitorial outdoors. This notion of 'an implicit agreement' is important. The more adults adopt a supervisory role the more likely it is that children will use them for routine help, to arbitrate disputes or even see them as people to avoid. This, in turn, can reinforce the monitorial role and a style of inter-action is set up, which, without reflection, can become a pattern that is difficult to change. Adults communicate powerful messages about what is expected, what is important and what is trivial. Often these messages are hidden and implicit, and therefore more pervasive in their impact.

All too often the key phrases of adult talk which dominate an outdoor play area can be negative phrases, such as 'Mind out. Be careful. Don't do that. Take turns. Put on your coat. Don't play on the grass'. The implicit message here is that, despite children's free choice of activity, adults remain firmly in control, judging the play, arbitrating in disputes, requiring permission, organizing activities and so on. Children have more control outdoors. There is more space and, therefore, greater physical freedom than indoors and children can, if they choose, ignore adults, move out of sight and avoid their requests in a way that is rarely possible indoors. Physically, children are often more competent than the adults and they can run faster, balance on high beams and manoevre through small spaces in ways that many adults can no longer do. It is perhaps not surprising that, when adults feel insecure and uncertain of their role, they try and reclaim some power and authority by adopting a controlling or monitorial role.

My work with a wide range of educators on in-service training courses suggests that there is considerable uncertainty about the role of the adult outdoors. They identify a tension between giving chil-dren the freedom to play yet also wanting to ensure children's safety and feeling pressurized to achieve curriculum outcomes. As a result the adult's role in children's play veers between under involvement as adults adopt a precautionary, supervisory role to over involve-ment as play is organized and directed with predetermined learning goals. As Malaguzzi has said, 'children are dangerously on the brink between presence that they want and repression that they don't want' (cited in Edwards *et al* 1993: 158).

Time

How time is organized can support or inhibit the quality of play outdoors. Rich, sustained play needs time. It has its own rhythm and momentum, sometimes intense, but short lived, sometimes extend-ing over many hours, days or even weeks. When children have long periods of time for play they can become more deeply involved and engrossed, and the stereotypical notion that young children do not stick at anything for long is often challenged. Laevers identified involvement and persistence as indicators of deep level learning (Pascal and Bertram 1997).

However, when adults control time by breaking it up into time-tabled slots or imposing restrictions on access to outdoors or are over zealous in the use of routines, children's play is disrupted or curtailed. Children themselves begin to devalue play knowing that there is little point in starting to build an elaborate scenario in the sand, for example, when the time outdoors is short lived. Involvement and persistence can be severely limited by seemingly arbitrary temporal restrictions.

Free movement indoors and out

When play can move freely between indoors and outdoors the pace becomes more relaxed and unhurried. Children can make choices as to where they play over time. Research by Bilton (2002) suggests that when rigid time barriers are removed the quality of the play and activity improves dramatically in the indoor, as well as the outdoor area as the pace is less frenetic and pressure on space reduced.

Free movement between indoors and outdoors allows play to evolve and helps children to make connections in their learning as the following examples illustrate:

Matthew and Aaron, aged 3, mixed water and sand together to make 'dinner'. They spread the mixture in some flat boxes and then fetched confetti and bottle tops from the nearby collage area to sprinkle on the top. These were then taken to the block area, slid inside a hollow block to cook and subsequently transported round the garden on trucks before being delivered to the home corner with a flourishing announcement of 'Pizza delivery!'

Quin, aged 4, played with the water wheel and gutters outdoors. He moved indoors to the construction table and made a wheel from construction straws. He then carried it to the water tray and poured water on the wheel, making it rotate. An adult suggested he find a way to support the axle which kept bending. He then ran outside to inspect the large water wheel then back to the construction table where he joined four wheels on one long axle. With great difficulty he carried this to the outside water tray so that the ends of the axle rested on the side of the tray. He then tested each wheel in turn under the water falling from the large water wheel.

These two examples illustrate how temporal and spatial fluidity can enable play to follow its own momentum and gain in complexity. The second example illustrates how the adult can extend the play. Rigid boundaries would have limited the scope of the play and foreclosed the possibilities of making connections.

Over-reliance on a rigid routine, clock watching, perpetually preparing for what comes next, change adults into controllers and monitors of time, rather than enablers. While some routine is necessary to provide a secure and predictable rhythm to the day, flexible and fluid organization of adults' time can protect space and time for children's play, and free it from unnecessary interruption. Research in reception classes by Rogers and Evans (2006) found that calling children away from play was the single most disruptive factor in the quality of children's role play. This, they argued, was because children need time to negotiate roles and develop their ideas but also because the social groups on which the play depended were terminated as a result of the disruption (Rogers and Evans 2006: 52).

There is also a reciprocal relationship between children's autonomy and adults' time. Strategies to promote children's independence and autonomy outdoors can reduce the management demands on adults. If children can find the resources they need, access appropriate clothing for different weather conditions and help each other with difficult tasks this frees time for adults to spend observing or interacting with children.

I watched a nursery adult supervising Ellie, aged 13 months. Ellie was intent on crawling towards an attractive stretch of grass. Every time she reached the grass the adult lifted her up and brought her back to the hard surface saying 'That's yucky wet grass'. This was repeated many times until Ellie gave up and turned her attention to something else. Had the adult allowed Ellie to get wet or provided appropriate clothes for crawling on the grass, time that was used for controlling and constraining could instead have been used for engaging with what it was that Ellie was interested in and for playfully exploring the wet grass together.

Setting up resources for play

Adults often spend considerable amounts of time setting up resources outdoors and arranging them in interesting configurations. A team of five practitioners I worked with on an in-service training course were shocked to discover that, collectively, they spent 20 hours a week setting out and putting away outdoor resources. While it is important that resources are well planned, look inviting and stimulate new ideas, nevertheless, it is hard for children to play with someone else's creations. In a small scale piece of action research we observed what children did with these carefully prepared scenarios. Invariably, within a very short time, set-ups had been dismantled or changed leading to a tension between adults and children as to the ownership of the play. For example:

Resources had been set out as a picnic with tablecloth, food, crockery and cutlery. A boy surreptitiously removed each plate, cup and saucer, one by one. He then carefully picked up the tablecloth, swirled it around his shoulder and ran off. The 'tablecloth' was, from his perspective, a favourite superhero cape. Staff unaware that this had happened despaired that their carefully set up activity had been 'ruined'. They were 'set up' for the day feeling annoyed and frustrated.

A well organized, but freely available picnic basket complete with tablecloth would perhaps have protected the play of children who wanted to play picnics, but also saved adults considerable amounts of time and avoided a boy having to retrieve, illicitly, the resources he needed.

This raises questions about why adults spend so long setting up elaborate play scenarios, such as building a train out of open-ended materials. This seems to negate the value of open-ended materials if they are prepared by adults, rather than transformed by children. Far more valuable would be if resources were attractively presented and the adult free to help children discuss, negotiate and problem solve how the train might be built. Questions such as 'Is this a good space?', 'What resources do we need?', 'What could we use for seats?' 'Do we need to build a station?' can act as prompts. Helping children to see the symbolic potential of features of the environment is an important strategy. 'Maybe these lines on the ground could be the train track'.

When provision is responsive to the previous day's observations, careful selection and arrangement of materials can be important ways for adults to invite new possibilities, suggest new combinations or encourage a continuation of play from the previous day. For example, after observing children's interest in rolling things down slopes, a range of planks, wheels, barrels and 'rollable' resources can develop and extend the play.

Figure 8.1 Responsive provision can extend children's interests and invite new possibilities.

Sensitive responsive relationships

Pascal and Bertram have identified three key principles which underpin effective adult engagement with children:

- **Sensitivity:** This is the sensitivity of the adult to the feelings and

well being of the child and includes elements of sincerity, empathy, responsiveness and affection.
- *Stimulation:* This is the way in which the adult intervenes in a learning process and the content of such interventions.
- *Autonomy:* This is the degree of freedom which the adult gives the child to experiment, make judgements, choose activities and express ideas. It also includes how the adult handles conflict, rules and behavioural issues (Pascal and Bertram 1997: 13).

Sensitive, responsive relationships underpin an effective adult role outdoors. Adults who listen to and engage with what children are trying to do can be rich catalysts for play. This is not easy and observations of interactions with children often reveal misunderstandings. Is the child painting a wall with a large paint brush and water (Figure 8.1) interested in covering the wall, filling in the rectangular patterns, pretending to be a painter and decorator, or exploring the evaporation of the water on the wall? Interaction based on assumptions as to what we think a child is doing is fraught with difficulty and leads to interactions that can be clumsy and intrusive.

Wells used the metaphor of throwing a ball to indicate the importance of the conversational exchange with young children:

> Like throwing a ball—first ensure that the child is ready with arms cupped to catch the ball, throw gently and accurately so that it lands squarely in the child's arms. When it is the child's turn to throw, the adult must be prepared to run wherever the ball goes.
>
> (Wells 1986: 50)

'Catching the ball that the children throw us' is a frequently used metaphor in Reggio Emilia, Italy and adult and teacher relationships are likened to a game of ping pong. 'Supportive adult relationships are based on keying in to the rhythm of the game and modeling an attitude of attention and care' (Edwards *et al* 1998: 181).

'Tuning in' to children is another metaphor that is frequently used, this time a musical one. Both of these metaphors emphasize the active, reciprocal, responsive role of the adult whose intention is to engage with, understand and respond to children. However, it needs to be recognized that understanding intentions and meeting minds is not easy. Even though we attempt to be in tune, the notes can be discordant and, at times, distinctly out of tune. Children can be tolerant of out of tune singing, but are dismissive if we start to sing a very different song in response to theirs. We can miss the ball occasionally, but if we do not return it the game is over. The important thing is the adults' intentions, the wanting and striving to understand combined with an informed understanding of young children's play and learning.

The following example illustrates the close reciprocal relationship between Angelina, a two-and-a-half-year-old toddler and Joan, his key person at nursery.

> They are talking with each other. Joan's gestures and Angelina's responses suggest that they are talking about the leaves blowing off the trees at the end of the garden. Angelina is running and excitedly watching the leaves spin down from the tree to the ground as the wind blows them off the branches . . . Joan offers her sustained and individual attention. Angelina seems to be having a very enjoyable, animated and exciting time catching the spinning leaves one by one. After catching each leaf, she runs back to Joan to be lifted up with her, and to look again over the wall.
>
> (Elfer *et al* 2003: 15)

Here, Joan and Angelina are in tune with each other. Joan responds to Angelina's interest and excitement in the falling leaves and they share it together. The close physical contact and, we can assume, the facial expressions and body language that accompany this, point to a close and intimate relationship, which is crucially important to Angelina's well being and her learning. The adult signals 'I'm interested in what you're interested in and what you're interested in is interesting'. Their attention on the blowing leaves is shared. The child's joy, excitement, physical activity, and need for physical closeness is acknowledged and reciprocated. The adult focuses on the moving, spinning leaves; she does not try and take over the interaction for a lesson on autumn leaves or to question Angelina's ability to count or name the colours of the leaves.

Such sensitive interaction contrasts sharply with the following edited observation by Tizard and Hughes (1984), where four-year-old Carol was excited about the wind blowing the buckets in the sand pit:

Child:	I'm telling Mummy that the buckets rolled away.
Teacher:	Pardon?
Child:	I'm telling Mummy that the buckets rolled away when we were not looking.
Teacher:	Are you?
Child:	Yeah.
Teacher:	That's nice.

Child: A-and the sand went a-all in my eyes.

Teacher: In your eyes? Were they sore? Are they still sore now? Oh you poor old thing. Do you think if you had a piece of apple, it would make them feel better?

[It was not until later at home talking with her mother that her real excitement was shared]

Child: Mummy I want to tell you something. And it's funny, um, the buckets rolled away and . . . and we weren't looking there . . . and we said . . . and we weren't able to catch the buckets.——

Mother: Were they rolling?

Child: Yeah Yeah. They were rolling . . . see, they were standing up, and we was not looking, cause, we was making sandcastles.

Mother: Mm.

Child: And then it tumbled over, the buckets, and then it went roll, roll, roll. Cause the wind blow huff.

Mother: Oh gosh. Very strong the wind isn't it.

(Tizard and Hughes 1984: 202–3)

As Tizard and Hughes point out the urgency and excitement of Carol's communication is missing in her interaction with her nursery teacher and she quickly enters into a dependent, help seeking relationship. There is a recognizable 'flat' tone to this interaction, which the researchers identified as characteristic of interactions where 'staff and children did not know each other very well' (1984: 202). However, it is not just the knowing it is the 'wanting to know' which is missing here. While we can hear the flatness of the tone of the conversation compared with the more animated and responsive tone of the mother's talk, I suspect that had this been a video, rather than an audio recording, the facial expression and body signals would have been as powerful, if not more powerful, in communicating the flatness of the tone.

We know from studies of interactions between parents and babies how, from birth, babies are tuned in to reading and responding to faces, and how quickly they learn to read signals of play from tone of voice and facial expressions. It is no good saying 'that's interesting' to a child if the facial expressions and body expressions indicate otherwise. Outdoors, when adults see their role as 'supervising' children, this sort of rather detached conversation can be prevalent as adults bend down to talk to children. Crouching or sitting can ensure effective face to face contact, a more equal balance of power, as well as allowing the adult the scope to scan the whole outdoor space when necessary.

The importance of close, intimate relationships can be seen in the example of sand cakes below. Pretend play is an important way that children seek out and maintain relationships with adults.

Sand cakes

A frequent occurrence in nursery settings is the almost ritual offerings of pretend food or drink, such as sand cakes. Typically, a plate of sand, a cup of water, or a container of soil and leaves is used by children to initiate an interaction with a particular adult. Although this also happens indoors, it is more prevalent outdoors where there is greater freedom of movement and opportunity to combine materials. Fascinated by the frequency and nature of these interactions I carried out a small piece of research (Tovey 1994). Children, I observed, were selective in the adult they chose often moving across a large area and by-passing more readily available adults nearby. Children initiated the play, signalling the pretence with grins and gleeful expressions. These were then 'read' and reciprocated by an adult to great amusement. All the adults I observed responded to the pretence but in very different ways.

Some not wanting to be drawn in deflected the child's approach, for example:

> I'm full up now; put it there and I'll eat it later with my cup of tea.
> Oh, another cake. I'll get fat.

Others responded by taking over the pretend offering and using it to interrogate the child, for example:

> Oh a cake. Lovely. Did you make it? What did you put in it? Flour, sugar?
> *Child nods.*
> Did you bake it? Where? In the oven? Oh lovely, you are clever. Does it need some icing on the top now?

Others responded to the pretence itself and elaborated it, for example:

> *Child:* Here's your cup of tea and here's your cake.
> *Adult:* Oh a cup of tea, thank-you. (*pretends to sip*). Ouch, it's hot.

Child: (*laughing*) Then blow on it then.

Adult: (*adult blows then takes another pretend sip*) Mmm delicious. Oh dear now I've spilt it all down me.

Child: (*pretending to mop up, laughing and scolding*). Look what you've done. You've spilt your tea! Now eat your cake. Ginger one

Adult: Mmm ginger cake. I love ginger cake. I'm going to eat it all up. Not a crumb left!

In this last example, the adult responded to the child's initiation and elaborated on the pretence, rather than seeking to take it over for her own purposes. This allowed the child to reciprocate the pretence. There was great glee when adults responded in this way especially when they made the appropriate exaggerated gestures of pretending to drink or eat, although some worried consternation if the actions seemed, rather too realistic, indicating that adults need to be very clear in signalling 'this is play'. Children often looked crestfallen when adults deflected the response, and there was some bewilderment when adults tried to use these offerings to take control and initiate a 'mini-lesson' or interrogate the child, thereby re-focusing the pretence back in reality. Children had after all merely filled a pot with sand or water, and these ritual offerings were quite different from the elaborate cooking of pretend food.

The shared conspiracy—we both know this is just sand, but we're both pretending it is food—generates much fun and laughter and establishes a close bond of friendship (Figure 8.2). However, as has been illustrated, adults' responses can either maintain or curtail such pretence and are, therefore, of crucial importance to the course of children's play and thinking, as well as to the quality of relationships. Adults working with the youngest children, when the ability to pretend and use an object or material to stand for another is just emerging, can see these small interactions and others like it as hugely significant in developing children's understanding of symbols.

Entering into children's worlds

The example of sand cakes might seem small and commonplace, but it illustrates the importance of being prepared to enter into the child's world and engage with the themes of the play, and crucially the intention behind the opening gesture. Research suggests that adults can find this difficult particularly when taking part in pretend play. Dunn (2004) for example observing children's pretend play at home noted that most adults who join in pretence usually do so in a rather

Figure 8.2 A meeting of minds. 'We both know it's sand but we're both pretending it's cake'.

boring, conventional way, focusing on the proper sequence of events for example when playing 'shops'. You're the person who takes the cash, so you'll take it from me . . . now you take my change . . . here's the way to the car. . . . (Dunn 2004: 25). Parents, unlike siblings rarely adopted a pretend identity or role. As Dunn pointed out, it is the shared enactment of joint pretence that is so powerful in developing relationships and friendships. While play with adults will never be the same as play between siblings and peers it would seem that the

Figure 8.3 By taking a role adults can extend the play from within the play frame.

capacity for adults to enter into the play allows the adult considerable influence in helping sustain the shared imagination, helping the play to continue and in helping less experienced players to access and remain in the play. An adult who takes on a pretend role announcing 'I'm the ticket collector and I'm going to check everyone's tickets' and then suddenly reverts to a teacherly role 'James you're being too noisy', breaks all the rules of play, whereas commenting from within the play frame such as 'we have some noisy passengers on the train. I need to call the transport police' opens up new roles and possibilities and is more likely to keep the play going.

Brostrom cautions against play becoming 'a mechanical and narrow reproduction of reality', instead it should be seen as 'a creative activity through which the child changes his or her surroundings, transforms knowledge and understanding and creates new insights through experience' (1998: 20). To be successful co-players adults also need to go well beyond reality and be willing to engage with the events as they unfold in play, helping children to transform space into dynamic and exciting new places.

Outdoors this requires much more than standing on the sidelines as spectators. As Kalliala points out, when adults are chatting together round the edges of the play area they are at a distance from the children, and observation is superficial and general, rather than deep and detailed. The themes of children's play culture she noted were tolerated by practitioners rather than engaged with:

> Barbies, Turtles, Biker Mice and Power Rangers are accepted but they are placed in a category in which adults do not have to know or appreciate anything about them even though they may be extremely important to the children. Sharing the children's cultural competence offers a good starting point for understanding the children's play.
>
> (Kalliaha 2006: 125)

Like Pascal and Bertram, Kalliala identifies sensitivity as a key principle in supporting children's play, but she also adds two more principles, the importance of informed observations of play and of knowing the world of children.

Helping children to negotiate and maintain their play ▮

Outdoors space is not static and predictable, but flexible and transformable, requiring considerable negotiation. Children also have to negotiate play in order to keep it going. Characters, plots and narratives have to be agreed and access to play negotiated. Inevitably, these negotiations can be precarious, particularly amongst inexperienced players, and play can easily break down. Adults have an important role in helping play to continue. Sometimes this involves protecting the space and time for play to continue and preventing intentional or unintentional interference, a frequent cause of play break down (Perry 2001). Trawick Smith (1998b) suggests that adults can also, at times, model negotiating strategies used by successful players, for example, announcing roles, checking agreement, clarifying events and so on. Adults can also help children develop ways to access play by observing the strategies that successful players use. For example, Corsaro (2003) observed that children use subtle strategies to access play. These included sitting close to the play and watching, encircling the area, adopting similar behaviour to the players or announcing similar actions. They rarely used the direct verbal request 'can I play?' as such a request was likely to be rejected. The least successful strategy is jumping in and disturbing the play, ignoring or misreading the current theme. Yet this can often be the approach that adults take, suggesting that not only does this interrupt play, but it also models an inappropriate strategy for children to use.

Of course, there are disputes and arguments in play. However, if adults intervene too quickly children never have the chance to communicate their grievance, and upset or try to resolve the 'stand-off' on their own. I watched two boys in a fierce argument over a favourite green wheeled vehicle known as 'the green bike'. It seemed that a fight might emerge, but I waited to see what might happen. After some loud and noisy exclamations of 'It's mine', 'no, it's mine I had it first', 'you're not my friend', 'well you're not my friend either', they realized that the vehicle moved if they both pushed with one leg. 'It can be both our bike', 'yeah it's both our bike'. They successfully propelled the vehicle around the play area, each pushing with one leg and steering with one hand. Intervening too quickly or imposing timed turn-taking can sometimes prevent these more idiosyncratic, but highly effective solutions to disputes to emerge. Knowledge of individual children and how they play is needed. With different children an adult might have intervened earlier maybe to protect a child who had difficulty accessing resources.

> Rushing in and rescuing children prematurely deprives them of the opportunity to flex their learning muscles and also to get used to the emotions which accompany such difficulties—frustration, confusion, apprehension and so on.
>
> (Claxton 1999: 265)

Supporting risky play

As Stephenson's (2003) research indicated, it is the adults' attitudes that make a difference to children's physical risk taking outdoors. Smith (1990, 1998) goes as far as to argue that risk defines our pedagogical relation to children. When adults are uncertain and anxious about children's safety outdoors they communicate this to children. Younger children especially look to adults for confirmation of whether something is safe to explore or to climb, and quickly 'read' the adults' assessment of the situation. If adults look permanently anxious then children either catch this fearfulness or choose to ignore it, but in so doing their ability to discriminate really risky situations is impeded.

Adults have a key role in supporting risk and challenge outdoors. This can include:

• Developing shared understandings and expectations within the staff team so that individuals feel supported and 'safe' to be risk takers themselves.
• Having realistically high expectations of what children can do. Knowing children well enough to make informed decisions as to when to intervene and when to stand back.

- Developing a positive disposition to challenge, seeing it as something to be relished, rather to be feared. Fostering children's autonomy and celebrating achievements, however small.
- Reflecting on gender differences in attitudes to risk. Is risk tolerated or encouraged more in boys' than in girls' play? Research referred to by Little (2006) suggests that often it is.
- Developing a language to talk about risk and safety, helping children to understand that being safe is under their control and to know how to do things safely. For example:
  - it's best to hold on now but when you feel safe enough you can try letting go;
  - it needs a lot of practice to be able to do that;
  - coming down backwards might be a safer way;
  - Josh found a very safe way of doing that shall we see how he did it?
  - that was good you remembered to check there was no one at the bottom of the slide before you pushed the box down.
- Being prepared to say a firm 'no that's dangerous because . . .' in the rare situations it is needed. Children can feel safer to take risks and be adventurous when there are clear boundaries and when they trust adults' judgement of a situation.
- Teaching skills that will help children to do things safely, for example, ways of controlling speed coming down a slide, safe ways of handling a saw at the woodwork bench or holding an insect, and so on.
- Modeling a flexible, innovative approach to situations, 'that's a good idea, let's try it', rather than the more rigid, cautious approach, 'we can't; there's no time; we don't move things; we mustn't make a mess; we're not allowed'.

Engaging in meaningful talk and interaction

Outdoors, as we have seen in previous chapters, is a rich source of surprise, curiosity, wonder, excitement and provides scope for imaginative exploration of ideas. How these are shared with adults is crucial. Coles (1996) reviewed research that suggests that what is most important in the behaviour of adults who are with young children is:

- sensitivity to the child's current state and an understanding of the child's level of ability and immediate interests;
- sensitivity to the meanings he or she is trying to communicate, and a desire to help and encourage interaction where both participants have equal space and discourse status;

- the ability to be a sympathetic listener rather than a propensity to dominate the situation and make it adult led;
- skill in responding to the meaning intended . . . and to have genuine concern to achieve a mutual understanding (Coles 1996: 10).

As the following example illustrates children's puzzled surprise can lead to extended and focused conversation where the source of puzzlement is jointly explored. Oliver (3 years and 10 months) found a conker in the nursery pond which he brought to show an adult.

Oliver: It's darker isn't it?
Adult: Mmm it's turned black.
Oliver: Why's it turned black?
Adult: Maybe because it's been in the water a long time.
Oliver: Yes, Yes, 'cos conkers are brown but this is black. I'm going to dry it on a tissue (*moves indoors*).
Oliver: It's still dark 'cos, 'cos if you put a brown conker in white water, it goes black doesn't it, 'cos brown and white make black don't they?
Adult: That's interesting. Well we could try that tomorrow with some paint—try mixing it up to see.
I think the conker is dark because it soaked up lots of water—look, like the tissue, where it's soaked up water it's gone darker.
Oliver: (*plays with tissue and conker in sink*)
If you put soap on it and put all water on it, it will go darker.

Here, Oliver initiates a conversation expressing surprise that a conker which he knew to be brown was now black. Such an observation illustrates the powerful curiosity and desire to make sense of a three-year-old's mind and how seemingly insignificant events outdoors can promote such enquiry. Adult and child negotiate meanings together that help shape the direction of his inquiry. The conversational structure clearly enhances rather than constrains the inquiry. Child initiates, adult responds and enlarges, child builds on answer and asks question, adult answers by reflecting on what is already known, child builds on answer and constructs his own explanation and so on. It illustrates Wells' (1986) emphasis on the importance of a conversational partner with whom meaning can be negotiated.

Sustained shared thinking

The observation of Oliver and the conker illustrates what Siraj-Blatchford *et al* (2002) have termed 'sustained shared thinking'. The REPEY (Researching Effective Pedagogy in the Early Years) project identified such conversation to be a particularly effective pedagogical strategy. Sustained shared thinking is defined as

> an episode in which two or more individuals 'work together' in an intellectual way to solve a problem, clarify a concept, evaluate activities or extend a narrative. Both parties must contribute to the thinking and it must develop and extend.
>
> (Siraj-Blatchford *et al* 2002: 8)

Each party therefore is engaging with the understanding of the other and learning is achieved through a process of reflexive co-construction. The REPEY project identified the most effective contexts for such shared thinking to be talk between an adult and one or two children. If the group was larger the adult talk was more likely to become monitorial. Significantly, the research identified that child-initiated play provided a rich context for such shared thinking. Unfortunately, there is no analysis on the frequency of episodes of sustained shared thinking in child initiated play outdoors.

Figure 8.4 Sustained shared attention leading to shared thinking about whether peppers on the capiscum plant can be eaten.

Thinking about thinking

The concepts of metacognition and meta play are important tools in helping us understand effective interaction in play. Metacognition or thinking about one's own thinking is a way of reflecting on and becoming more aware of one's own processes of thinking. Research suggests that if adults use a range of 'thinking words', such as think, know, remember, expect, consider, reconsider, wonder, guess, imagine, decide in everyday conversation then children themselves come to think and talk like this (Astington 1994). The following observation and analysis of play outdoors illustrates this.

A group of four-year-olds were using milk crates and gutters to transport water from one side of the play area to another. They encountered many problems as they tried to construct gradients to allow the water to flow. The play, which had no end point, but ebbed and flowed, lasted for two days. Two hours of the play was video-taped. Georgina was involved in the whole episode. A transcript of talk initially appeared unpromising. Action dominated and the conversation was context bound and elliptical. For example:

Georgina:	Put that one there
Adult:	Do you mean here?
Georgina:	No, that blue one
Adult:	Like this?
Georgina:	No like this.

Clearly, when both children and adults are acting together there is little need for elaborated talk although it illustrates how for most of the time Georgina held the conversational initiative.

However, closer examination of the full transcript revealed considerable evidence of Georgina's emerging awareness of her own thinking skills. For example, the phrase 'I've got a good idea' was repeated a staggering seventeen times and there were numerous repetitions of 'that was a good idea wasn't it?' Other phrases included:

- Oh, it didn't work; I don't know what to do now.
- That's no good; I think I need to find a long one to fit here . . .
- Ooh I can't think. You help me now.
- We did that afore. Oh no I forgot about that.
- We have to change it—that's no good an idea.

While much of her action was trial and error she clearly perceived herself as someone with good ideas, who was thinking, puzzling, reflecting, checking, correcting and acknowledging her need for help. In turn the adult responded to this with such phrases as

- What do you *think* of that?
- I don't *understand*, do you mean . . .?
- Scott *thought*. . . . What do you *think*? Do you *think* that's a good *idea*?
- *Remember* when we did that before.
- Can you *guess* . . .
- Have you *checked* if . . .
- I *wonder* what would happen if we . . .
- Oh dear I *thought* that might happen. Maybe we have to *re-think* that idea.

This type of interaction, when the adult confirms and enlarges the scope of the child's intentions and responds **as though** Georgina has plans, intentions, ideas, strategies and thoughts, and can predict, check, guess and wonder about what is happening is clearly crucially important for developing awareness of children's thinking. As Meadows and Cashdan state 'thinking about your thinking seems to be an effective way of getting better at it and also to be a source of self-confidence' (1988: 56). It is also inherently respectful of children's ideas, purposes and intentions.

Feeling puzzled, baffled or, at times, wrong is as important as feeling competent, providing the setting is supportive. Holding back an instinctive desire to help can be important in allowing children time to see mistakes and to reveal their understanding thereby allowing adults a chance to intervene in a meaningful way.

Questioning

I have a powerful recollection of being four and taken round the school garden by a well meaning teacher. We stopped to look at the flowers. 'What's that called?' she asked pointing to a rose. I remember thinking 'Why is she asking me? Doesn't she know it's a rose?' In this moment of confusion I replied 'I don't know'. I can still feel the mixture of indignation and humiliation as she replied 'it's called a rose, dear'. Young children are often confused by a style of interaction where questions are not for puzzling and for finding out, but are used for testing. Power is located with the adult and children begin to see their role as answering, rather than asking questions.

Outdoors, however, children have an effective strategy in response to adults' persistent questions, they can move away! In a two-hour videotape of outdoor play in an excellent nursery setting I noted eight examples of children simply ignoring the adults' questions, particularly when they were difficult ones such as 'how does the pulley work? Where did the puddle go?' When children ignore adults this in turn can cause adults to feel ineffective in their role.

Open-ended wondering questions such as 'I wonder why that happened, what made you think that, I wonder what might happen if . . .?' invite speculation and consideration. They pose a question, but do not demand a response. Curiosity is the key. Children need to believe that adults are interested in their ideas, and that a question is a genuine attempt to understand their ideas or to clarify their thinking. Well timed questions, which are relevant to the focus of children's attention, can take their enquiries forward. For example, a teacher in Reggio Emilia, Italy posed the question 'can you make a shadow go away?' This led to sustained investigation as children tested their ideas—lying on the ground, trying to cover the shadow with stones, then with a sheet before concluding 'it won't cover up' (Reggio Children 1996: 122).

The REPEY research (Siraj-Blatchford *et al* 2002) confirms the importance of open-ended, rather than closed questions in effective pedagogy. However, even in excellent settings such questions were rare, only 5 per cent of the total number of questions asked compared with 34 per cent of closed questions. This concurs with the finding of previous studies (Tizard and Hughes 1984; Wells 1986) and indicates that adults' use of questions is still highly problematic.

Children's questions reveal puzzlement, surprise and a striving to understand. Forming a question is an important way of focusing and communicating the source of puzzlement to adults. Outdoor environments can be a rich source of puzzlement for young children, and this can be seen in the surprised and curious expressions and explorations of the youngest children, and the why questions of older children:

- Who waters the trees and how did they get right up there to water them?
- Why is all that sugar on the cars? [*A child seeing snow for the first time*]
- Why is there glass on the pond? [*A child looking at ice*]
- How do worms breathe under there? Why don't they sufferate?
- How do snails eat lettuce when they haven't got any teeth?

In these examples children are identifying confusion between what they know and what they see. Teeth are for eating, so how can a snail eat when he hasn't any teeth? Sometimes children pose and answer their own questions, showing the ability to both frame a question and interrogate their own experience in search of an answer. The adult then becomes an important sounding board for reflection. Pauses and silences allow 'thinking time' for children.

- How did that big ice get in there [*a plastic bottle*]. Did it melt first?
- Why does it [*a duckling*] drink water like that, with its neck like that? Why doesn't it drink like a cat? I know 'cos it hasn't got a tongue.

However, questions are not just about the physical world. Children are curious about the world of people, emotions, how others think and behave:

- When I say yes, Alex says no. Why does he do that?
- Why do teachers keep saying 'you can't climb over the top [*of the climbing frame*] when I can!'
- Why do men hoover the grass? [*watching gardeners mow the grass*]

'Why' questions can also be found in pretend play and children, particularly those at the upper end of the early years, frequently challenge inconsistencies in the play script:

- Why is he going to bed? He hasn't had his dinner yet.
- How come we're sailing? We can't be sailing, I haven't pulled the anchor.

If children's puzzling questions are to thrive, there has to be more than a rich environment. There have to be adults who show their interest in children's questions, who invite such questions by being open and available, who treat them as worthy of interest and respect, and who are willing to respond in a way that engages the child or group of children, in further enquiry.

Observing, supporting and extending play

The essence of adults and children developing play together is for the adult to 'observe, support and extend the play' (Bruce 1987). Observation means using theory and research to inform both on the spot and reflective understanding about play between adults and children. Supporting begins where the child is and with what the child can do. Extending might be to give help with physical materials, create space, give time, dialogue

Figure 8.5 An adult supporting and extending play. She poses a question 'I wonder what will happen if I let go?' Later they discuss ways of making the structure more stable.

and converse about the play idea, or help with access strategies for the child to enter into play with other children. Extending also involves sensitivity and adding appropriately stimulating material provision and the encouragement of the child's autonomous learning.

(Bruce 1997: 97)

Conclusion

Earlier in this chapter we looked at the metaphors of 'throwing a ball' and 'tuning in'. Loris Malaguzzi, architect of the thinking which underpins the approach in Reggio Emilia, Italy, used a theatrical metaphor, summarized here by Rinaldi.

> We need a teacher who is sometimes the director, sometimes the set designer, sometimes the curtain and the backdrop, and sometimes the prompter ... who is the electrician, who dispenses the paints and who is even the audience—the audience who watches, sometimes claps, sometimes remains silent, full of emotion, who sometimes judges with scepticism, and at other times applauds with enthusiasm.
>
> (Malaguzzi, cited in Rinaldi 2006: 73)

We can add to this the notion of the adult as actor 'involved in an element of improvisation, a sort of "playing by ear," an ability to take stock of a situation, to know when to move and when to stay still, that no formula or recipe can replace' (Rinaldi 2006: 73). If we also accept that the 'stage' for play is not fixed and static, but constantly transforming, then we can begin to see the complex, multi-faceted role of the adult engaged in supporting children's play outdoors. This requires knowledge, skill as well as a willingness to acknowledge mistakes, and a striving to develop one's own understanding and practice.

This importance of reflection has been emphasised throughout this book. The nursery outdoor play area has been part of the nursery tradition, a rich inheritance of diverse ideas, approaches and practices. But like all traditions it can be taken for granted, ignored or misunderstood. We have a responsibility to reflect critically on this tradition and the ideas of the pioneers for it is by returning to and examining their thinking that we can enrich and sharpen our own. Equally significant is the growing cross fertilisation of ideas as the more rigid professional boundaries between play workers, early childhood educators, health professionals, landscape architects, planners and health and safety officers are starting to be crossed and opportunities for debate and dialogue emerging. Cross disciplinary study is also opening up ideas in exciting ways and disciplines such as social geography, health, sociology, landscape architecture can offer particular insights into young children's play outdoors and enrich our understanding. But underpinning our approach to play outdoors must be a debate as to what sort of outdoor spaces we want for children and reflection on the values which underpin them.

Without such reappraisal we are in danger of losing a rich inheritance and burying it under layers of tarmac and rubberised safety surfaces, denying children the opportunities to learn through rich play, adventure, risk and challenge.

BIBLIOGRAPHY

Adams, S., Alexander, E., Drummond, M. & Moyles, J. (2004) *Inside the Foundation Stage. Recreating the Reception Year*. London: Association of Teachers and Lecturers.

Allen, M. (Lady Allen of Hurtwood) (1965) *Design for Play: the youngest children*. London: Housing Centre Trust.

Allen, M. (Lady Allen of Hurtwood) (1968) *Planning for Play*. London: Thames & Hudson.

Armitage, M. (1999) *What Do You Mean You Don't Like It? Interpreting Children! Perceptions of the Playground as an Aid to Designing Effective Play Space*, a paper for the 2nd International Toy Research Conference, Halmstad, Sweden.

Armitage, M. (2001) The ins and outs of school playground play: children's use of 'play places'. In: J. C. Bishop & M. Curtis (Eds) *Play Today in the Primary School Playground*. Buckingham: Open University Press.

Armitage, M. (2005) The influence of school architecture and design on the outdoor play experience within the primary school. *Pedagogica Historica*, 41, Nos 4 & 5, August, 535–553.

Astington, J. (1994) *The Child's Discovery of the Mind*. London: Fontana Press.

Athey, C. (1990) *Extending Thought in Young Children*. London: Paul Chapman.

Bachelard, G. (1994) *The Poetics of Space: the classic look at how we experience intimate places*. Boston: Beacon Press.

Ball, D. (2002) *Playgrounds—Risks, Benefits and Choices*. Norwich: Health and Safety Executive, HMSO.

Barbour, A. (1999) The impact of playground design on the play behaviours of children with differing levels of physical competence. *Early Childhood Research Quarterly*, 14, 75–98.

Bateson, G. (1956) The message 'This is play'. In: B. Schaffner (Ed.) *Group Processes*. New York: Josiah Macy

Beard, R. (Ed.) (1995) *Rhyme, Reading and Writing*. London: Hodder & Stoughton.

Beck, U. (1993) *Risk Society: towards a new modernity*. London: Sage Publications.

Berlin, I. (1969) *Four Essays on Liberty*. Oxford: Oxford University Press.

Bilton, H. (2002) *Outdoor Play in the Early Years: management and innovation*. London: David Fulton Publishers.

Bilton, H. (2004) *Playing Outside: activities, ideas and inspiration for the early years*. London: David Fulton.

Bilton, H. (Ed.) (2006) *Learning Outdoors: improving the quality of young children's play outdoors*. London: David Fulton Publishers.

Bishop, J. C. & Curtis, M. (2001) *Play Today in the Primary School Playground*. Buckingham: Open University Press.

Bixler, R. D, Carlisle, C. L., Hammitt, W. E. & Floyd, M. F. (1994) Observed fears and discomforts among urban students on field trips to wildland areas. *Journal of Environmental Educational*, 26, No. 1, 24–33.

Blakemore, S. & Frith, U. (2005) *The Learning Brain*. Oxford: Blackwell.

Bloom, A. (2006) Infants on the treadmill. *The Guardian*, 20 October.

Bradburn, E. (1989) *Margaret McMillan. Portrait of a Pioneer*. London: Routledge.

Brehony, K. (2004) *Working at Play and Playing at Work? A Froebelian Paradox Re-examined*, Inaugural Lecture, Roehampton University.

British Medical Association (2005) *Preventing Childhood Obesity*. London: BMA.

Broadhead, P. (2004) *Early Years Play and Learning: developing social skills and cooperation*. London: Routledge.

Brostrom, S. (1998) Frame play in early childhood education. *International Journal of Early Childhood*, 30, 27–35.

Brown, F. (Ed.) (2003) *Playwork: theory and practice*. Buckingham: Open University Press.

Brown, J. & Burger, C. (1984) Playground designs and preschool children's behaviour. *Environment and Behaviour*, 16(5), 599–626.

Bruce, T. (1984) A Froebelian Looks at Montessori's Work. *Early Child Development and Care*, 19(3), 151–173.

Bruce, T. (1991) *Time to Play in Early Childhood Education*. London: Hodder & Stoughton.

Bruce, T. (1997) Adults and children developing play together. *European Early Childhood Education Research Journal*, 5(1), 89–99.

Bruce, T. (2004) *Developing Learning in Early Childhood*. London: Paul Chapman Publishing.

Bruner, J. S (1980) *Under Five in Britain*. London: Grant McIntyre Ltd

Burke, C. (2005) 'Play in Focus': children researching their own spaces and places for play. *Children, Youth and Environments*, 15, 27–53.

Caillois, R. (2001) *Man, Play and Games* (M. Barash, Trans.) Urbana: University of Illinois Press.

Callaway, G. (2005) *The Early Years Curriculum: a view from outdoors*. London: David Fulton Publishers.

Carrell, S. (2006) Pioneer nursery stays open outdoors in all weathers. *The Guardian*, 30 October.

Carson, R. (1998) *The Sense of Wonder*. New York: HarperCollins.

Ceppi, G. & Zini, M. (Eds) (1998) *Children, Spaces, Relations: meta-project for an environment for young children*. Milan: Domus Academy Research Centre & Reggio Children.

Chawla, L. (1990) Ecstatic places. *Children's Environments Quarterly*, 7(4), 18–23.

Chilton, S. (2003) Adventure playgrounds in the twentieth century. In: F. Brown (Ed.) *Playwork*. Buckingham: Open University Press.

Chukovsky, K. (1968) *From Two to Five*. Berkeley: University of California Press.

Clark, A. (2005) Talking and listening to children. In: M. Dudek (Ed.) *Children's Spaces*. London: Elsevier.

Clark, A. & Moss, P. (2001) *Listening to Young Children. The Mosaic Approach*. London: National Children's Bureau.

Clark, A. & Moss, P. (2006) *Spaces to Play. More Listening to Young Children Using the Mosaic Approach*. London: National Children's Bureau.

Claxton, G. (1999) *Wise up: the challenge of life long learning*. London: Bloomsbury Publishing plc.

Cobb, E. (1977) *The Ecology of Imagination in Childhood*. London: Routledge and Kegan Paul.

Cohen, B. (Ed.) (2005) Space Standard in Services for Young Children. *Children in Europe*, 8, 6–7.

Coles, M (1996) The magicfying glass: what we know of classroom talk in the early years. In: N. Hall and J. Martello (Eds) *Listening to Children Think: exploring talk in the early years*. London: Hodder & Stoughton.

Corsaro, W. (2003) *We're Friends Right? Inside Kids' Culture*. Washington, DC: Joseph Henry Press.

Crystal, D. (1998) *Language Play*. London: Penguin.

De Carlo, G. (1974) Why/how to build school buildings. In G. Coates (Ed) *Alternative Learning Environments*. Stroudsburg, PA: Dowden, Hutchinson & Ross.

Department for Education and Skills (2007) *Practice Guidance for the Foundation Stage*. Nottingham: DfES Publications.

Dietz, W. (2001) The obesity epidemic in young children: reduce television viewing and promote playing. *British Medical Journal*, 10 February.

Dixon, J. & Day, S. (2004) Secret places: 'You're too big to come in here'. In: H. Cooper (Ed.) *Exploring Time and Place Through Play*. London: David Fulton Publishers.

Donaldson, M. (1978) *Children's Minds*. Glasgow: Fontana/Collins.

Douglas, M. (1992) *Risk and Blame: essays in cultural theory*. London: Routledge.

Doyle, J. (2005) Nature makes the best teacher and classroom. *Early Years Educator*, 8, No. 3, *Forest Schools Supplement*, ii–x.

Drummond, M. J. (1995) Foreword. In: S. Hogan, & A. Hedley (Eds) *'Can I Play Out?' Outdoor Play in the Early Years*. Bradford: Bradford Education.

Drummond, M. (1999) Another way of seeing: perceptions of play in a Steiner kindergarten. In: L. Abbott & H. Moylett (Eds) *Early Education Transformed*. London: Falmer Press.

Drummond, M. (2000) Comparisons in early years education: history, fact and fiction. *Early Childhood Research and Practice*, 2(1). Available at: http://ecrp.uiuc.edu/vzni/drummond.html (accessed 8 August 2006).

Dudek, M. (2005) *Children's Spaces*. Oxford: Elsevier Architectural Press.

Dunn, J. (1988) *The Beginnings of Social Understanding*. Oxford: Blackwell.

Dunn, J. (2004) *Children's Friendships: the beginning of intimacy*. Oxford: Blackwell Publishing.

Dweck, C. (2000) *Self Theories: their role in motivation, personality and development*. Hove: Psychology Press.

Edgington, M. (2003) *The Great Outdoors: developing children's learning through outdoor provision*. London: British Association of Early Childhood Education.

Edwards, C., Gandini, L. & Forman, G. (1998) *The Hundred Languages of Children. The Reggio Emilia Approach—Advanced Reflections*. Greenwich: Ablex.

Einstein, A. (1984) Albert Einstein. In: M. Booth (Ed.) *What I Believe*. London: Firethorn Press.

Elfer, P., Goldschmied, E. & Selleck, D. (2003) *Key Persons in the Nursery: building relationships for quality and provision*. London: David Fulton Publishers.

Factor, J. (2004) Tree stumps, manhole covers and rubbish tins. The invisible play-lines of a primary school. *Childhood*, 11, Issue 2, 142–154.

Faux, K. (2005) At full stretch. *Nursery World*, 17th February.

Fjortoft, I. (2001) The natural environment as a playground for children: the impact of outdoor play activities in pre-primary school children. *Early Childhood Education*, 29(2), 111–117.

Fjortoft, I (2004) Landscapes as playscape: the effects of natural environments on children's play and motor development. *Children Youth and Environments*, 14(2), 21–44. Available at: http://www.colorado.edu/journals/cye/ (accessed 10 August 2006).

Fox, L. (2005) Children too noisy to play outdoors. *Nursery World*, 17 August.

Freire, P. (1972) *Pedagogy of the Oppressed*. London: Sheed and Ward.

Furedi, F. (2002) *Culture of Fear: risk taking and the morality of low expectations*. London: Continuum.

Garrick, R. (2004) *Playing Outdoors in the Early Years*. London: Continuum.

Garvey, C. (1991) *Play*. Glasgow: Fontana Press/HarperCollins.

Gibbs, J. (2005) *Are Children the Invisible Citizens of Public Life? An Examination of Changing Perceptions of Childhood in Contemporary Society*. Unpublished BA Early Childhood Studies Dissertation, Roehampton University, London.

Gill, T. (2004) Bred in captivity. *The Guardian*, 20 September.

Gill, T. (2005) In need of an un level playing field. *The Guardian*, 3rd August.

Gill, T. (2006a) Home zones in the UK: history, policy and impact on children and youth. *Children, Youth and Environments*, 16, 90–103.

Gill, T. (2006b) The play's the thing. *The Guardian*, 15 June.

Goddard Blythe, S. (2004) *The Well Balanced Child: movement and early learning*. Stroud: Hawthorn Press.

Golby, M. (1988) Traditions in primary education. In: M. Clarkson (Ed.) *Emerging Issues in Primary Education*. Lewes: Falmer Press.

Goldschmied, E. & Jackson, S. (2004) *People Under Three: young children in day care*, 2nd edn. London: Routledge.

Goldstein, G. (1992) *War Toys: a review of research*. London: Toy and Hobby Association.

Goleman, D. (1996) *Emotional Intelligence: why it can matter more than IQ*. London: Bloomsbury.

Gopnik, A., Meltzoff, A. & Kuhl, P. (1999) *How Babies Think*. London: Phoenix.

Greater London Authority (2004) *State of London's Children*. London: Greater London Authority.

Greenland, P. (2006) Physical development. In: Bruce, T (Ed.) *Early Childhood: a guide for students*. London: Sage Publications.

Greenman, J. (1988) *Caring Spaces, Learning Spaces*. Redmond: Exchange Press Inc.

Gullov, E. (2003) Creating a natural place for children: an ethnographic study of Danish kindergartens. In: K. Olwig & E. Gullov (Eds) *Children's Places: cross-cultural perspectives*. London: Routledge.

Gussin Paley, V. (1986) On listening to what the children say. *Harvard Educational Review*, 56(2), 122–131.

Gussin Paley, V. (1990) *The Boy Who Would Be a Helicopter*. London: Harvard University Press.

Haas, M. (1996) Children in the junkyard. *Childhood Education*, 71(4), 212–216.

Heft, H. (1988) Affordances of children's environments: a functional approach. *Children's Environments*, 5(3), 29–37.

Hendricks, B. (2003) *Designing for Play*. Aldershot: Ashgate Publishing Ltd.

Henniger, M. (1994) Adult perceptions of favorite childhood play experiences. *Early Child Development and Care*, 99, 23–30.

Herrington, S. (1997) The received view of play and the subculture of infants. *Landscape Journal*, 16, 149–160.

Herrington, S. (2001) Kindergarten garden pedagogy from Romanticism to Reform. *Landscape Journal*, 20, 30–34.

Herrington, S. (2004) Muscle memory: reflections on the North American schoolyard. In: H. M. Goelman and S. Ross (Eds) *Multiple Lenses Multiple Images*. Toronto: University of Toronto Press.

Herrington, S. (2005a) The sustainable landscape. In: M. Dudek (Ed.) *Children's Spaces*. London: Elsevier/Architectural Press.

Herrington, S. (2005b) Landscapes at childcare centres: dos and don'ts. *Landscapes/Paysages*, 7(2), 16–20.

Hicks, J. & Hicks, J. (2005) Razor blades and teddy bears—the health and safety protocol. In: M. Dudek (Ed.) *Children's Spaces*. Oxford: Elsevier/Architectural Press.

Hillman, M., Adams, S. & Whitelegg, J. (1990) *One False Move: a study of children's independent mobility*. London: Policy Studies Institute.

HMI (1989) *A Survey of the Quality of Education for Four Year Olds in Primary Classes*. London: DES.

Holland, P. (2003) *We Don't Play with Guns Here. War Weapon and Superhero Play in the Early Years*. Maidenhead: Open University Press.

Holman, B. (2001) *Champions for Children, the Lives of Modern Child Care Pioneers*. Bristol: Policy Press.

Huizinga, J. (1950) *Homo Ludens: a study of the play element in culture*. London: Beacon Press.

Hutt, S., Tyler, S., Hutt, C. & Christopherson, H. (1989) *Play Exploration and Learning: a natural history of the pre-school*. London: Routledge.

International Obesity Taskforce. (2002) *Obesity in Europe: the case for action*. London: IOTF.

Isaacs, S. (1929) *The Nursery Years. The Mind of the Child from Birth to Six Years*. London: Routledge & Kegan Paul.

Isaacs, S. (1930) *Intellectual Growth in Young Children*. London: Routledge & Kegan Paul.

Isaacs, S. (1932) *The Children We Teach*. London: Routledge & Kegan Paul.

Jackson, S. & Scott, S. (1999) Risk anxiety and the social construction of childhood. In: D. Lupton (Ed.) *Risk and Sociocultural Theory: new directions and perspectives*. Cambridge: Cambridge University Press.

Jenkinson, S. (2001) *The Genius of Play: celebrating the spirit of childhood*. Stroud: Hawthorn Press Ltd.

Jotangia, D., Moody, A., Stamatakis, E. & Wardle, H. (2007) *Health Survey for England: obesity in children under eleven*. London: Department of Health.

Jilk, B. (2005) Place making and change in learning environments. In: M. Dudek (Ed.) *Children's Spaces*. Oxford: Elsevier Architectural Press.

Kalliala, M. (2006) *Play Culture in a Changing World*. Maidenhead: Open University Press.

Katz, L. (1995) *Talks with Teachers of Young Children*. Norwood: Ablex.

Keating, E. (2002) Unpublished Essay. London: Roehampton University.

Kirby, M. (1989) Nature as refuge in children's environments. *Children's Environments Quarterly*, 6(1). 7–12.

Kylin, M. (2003) Children's dens, *Children, Youth and Environments*. Available at: http://colorado.edu/journals/cye (accessed 9 August 2006).

Laris, M. (2005) Designing for play. In: M. Dudek (Ed.) *Children's Spaces*. London: Elsevier/Architectural Press.

Leibschner, J. (1992) *A Child's Work: freedom and guidance in Froebel's educational theory and practice*. Cambridge: Lutterworth Press.

Lilley, I. (1967) *Friedrich Froebel: a selection from his writings*. Cambridge: Cambridge University Press.

Lindon, J. (1999) *Too Safe for their Own Good? Helping Children Learn about Risk and Lifeskills*. London: National Early Years Network.

Little, H. (2006) Children's risk taking behaviour: implications for early childhood policy and practice. *International Journal of Early Years Education*, 14(2), 141–154.

Louv, R. (2005) *Last Child in the Woods: saving our children from nature-deficit disorder*. New York: Algonquin Books.

Lupton, D. (Ed.) (1999) *Risk and Sociocultural Theory: new directions and perspectives*. Cambridge: Cambridge University Press.

Lupton, D. (2006) *Risk*. London: Routledge.

Malaguzzi, L. (1993) History, ideas and basic philosophy: an interview with Lella Gandini. In: C. Edwards, L. Gandini & G. Forman (Eds) *The Hundred Languages of Children*. Norwood: Ablex.

Maynard, T. & Waters, J. (2006) Learning in the outdoor environment: a missed opportunity, paper given at the 16th ECCERA Conference, Democracy and Culture in Early Childhood Education, Reykjavik, 31 August to 2 September 2006.

McAuley, H. & Jackson, P. (1992) *Educating Young Children: a structural approach*. London: David Fulton Publishers in Association with the Roehampton Institute.

McConville, B. (1997) Happy campers. *Nursery World*, 16 January.

McMillan, M. (1919) *The Nursery School*. London: Dent.

McMillan, M. (1930) *The Nursery School*. London: Dent.

Meadows, S. & Cashdan, A. (1988) *Helping Children Learn*. London: David Fulton.

Melville, S. (2004) *Places for Play*. London: Playlink.

Mental Health Foundation. (1999) *Bright Futures: promoting children and young people's mental health*. London: Mental Health Foundation.

Montessori, M. (1920) *The Montessori Method*. London: Heinemann.

Montessori, M. (1949) *The Absorbent Mind*. Madras: Kalakshetra Publications.

Montessori, M. (1983) *The Secret of Childhood*. London: Sangam Books Ltd.

Montessori, M. (1989) *The Formation of Man*. Oxford: Clio Press Ltd.

Moore, R. C. (1986) *Childhood's Domain: play and place in child development*. London: Croom Helm.

Moore, R. C. (1989) Plants as play props. *Children's Environments Quarterly*, 6(1), 1–4

Moore, R. C. (1995) Children's gardening: first steps towards a sustainable future. *Children's Environments*, 12, 222–232.

Moore, R. C. & Wong, H. H. (1997) *Natural Learning: creating environments for rediscovering Nature's way of teaching*. Berkley: MIG Communications.

Morrongiello, B. A. & Hogg, K. (2004) Mothers' responses to sons and daughters engaging in injury-risk behaviors on a playground: implications for sex differences in injury rates. *Journal of Experimental Child Psychology*, 76, 89–103.

Moss, P. & Petrie, P. (2002) *From Children's Services to Children's Spaces*. London: Routledge.

Mountain, J. (2001) In the zone. *National Early Years Network*, issue 81, 14–15.

Moyles, J. (Ed.) (1989) *Just Playing? The Role and Status of Play in Early Childhood Education*. Buckingham: Open University Press.

Murray, R. & O'Brien, E (2006) *'Such Enthusiasm—A Joy to See'. An Evaluation of Forest Schools in England*. Report to the Forestry Commission by NEF (New Economic Foundation) and Forest Research. Farnham: Forest Research.

Nabhan, G. (1994) A child's sense of wildness. In: G. Nabhan & S. Trimble (Eds) *The Geography of Childhood: why children need wild spaces*. Boston: Beacon Press.

Navarra, J. (1955) *The Development of Scientific Concepts in a Young Child*. New York: Teachers College Press.

Nebelong, H. (2004) Nature's playground. *Green Places*, 5, 28–31.

Nicholson, S. (1971) 'How NOT to cheat children: the theory of loose parts. *Landscape Architecture*, October, 30–34.

Norman, N. (2003) *An Architecture of Play: a survey of London's adventure playgrounds*. London: Four Corners Books.

Opie, I. & Opie, P. (1959) *The Lore and Language of Schoolchildren*. London: Oxford University Press.

Opie, I. & Opie, P. (1969) *Children's Games in Street and Playground*. London: Oxford University Press.

Ouvry, M. (2000) *Exercising Muscles and Minds. Outdoor Play and the Early Years Curriculum*. London: National Early Years Network.

Palmer, S. (2006) *Toxic Childhood*. London: Orion Books.

Pascal, C., & Bertram, T. (1997) *Effective Early Learning*. London: Hodder and Stoughton.

Pellegrini, A. & Smith, P. (1998) Physical activity play: the nature and function of a neglected aspect of play. *Child Development*, 69, 577–598.

Penn, H. (2005a) *Understanding Early Childhood: issues and controversies*. Maidenhead: Open University Press.

Penn, H. (2005b) Spaces without children. In: M. Dudek (Ed.) *Children's Spaces*. London: Elsevier.

Perry, J. (2001) *Outdoor Play. Teaching Strategies with Young Children*. New York: Teachers College Press.

Play Safety Forum (2002) *Managing Risk in Play Provision: a position statement*. London: Children's Play Council.

Polakow, V. (1992) *The Erosion of Childhood*. Chicago: University of Chicago Press.

Proud, C. (1999) In: Sightlines Initiative (Eds) *Time Out in the Woodland*. Newcastle: Sightlines Initiative.

Pullman, P. (2005) Common sense has much to learn from moonshine. *The Guardian*, 22 January.

QCA (2000) *Curriculum Guidance for the Foundation Stage*. London: QCA/DfEE.

Raymund, J. F (1995) From barnyards to backyards: an exploration through adult memories and children's narratives in search of an ideal playscape. *Children's Environments*, 12(3), 134–161.

Reggio Children (1996) *The Hundred Languages of Children*, exhibition catalogue. Reggio Emilia: Reggio Children.

Reifel, S. & Yeatman, J. (1993) From category to context: reconsidering classroom play. *Early Childhood Education Research Quarterly*, 8, 347–367.

Reilly, J., Methven, E., McDowell, Z., Hacking, B., Alexander, D., Stewart, L., *et al.* (2003) Health Consequences of Obesity. *Lancet*, January 2003.

Rich, D., Casanova, D., Dixon, D., Drummond, M., Durrant, A. & Myer, C. (2005) *First Hand Experience: what matters to children*. Suffolk: Rich Learning Opportunities.

Rinaldi, C. (2006) *In Dialogue with Reggio Emilia. Listening, Researching and Learning*. Abingdon: Routledge.

Rissotto, A. & Giuliani, V. (2006) Learning neighbourhood environments: the loss of experience in a modern world. In: C. Spencer & M. Blades (Eds) *Children and their Environments: learning using and designing spaces*. Cambridge: Cambridge University Press.

Rogers, S. & Evans, J. (2006) Playing the game? Exploring role play from children's perspectives. *European Early Childhood Education Research Journal*, 14(1) 43–56.

Rogers, S., Woods, P. & Evans, J. (2005) *Role Play in Reception Classes: pupil and teacher perspectives*, ESRC End of Award Report. Available at: www.esrcsocietytoday.ac.uk/ESRCinfoCenter/ViewAwardPage.aspx (accessed 8 August 2006).

Rubin, Z. (1983) The skills of friendship. In: M. Donaldson, R. Grieve & C. Pratt (Eds) *Early Childhood Development and Education*. Oxford: Blackwell.

Ryder Richardson, G. (2006) *Creating a Space to Grow: developing your outdoor learning environment*. London: David Fulton Publishers.

School Curriculum and Assessment Authority (1996) *Desirable Learning Outcomes for Children Entering Compulsory Education*. London: SCAA.

Sestini, E. (1987) The quality of the learning experiences of four-year-olds in nursery and infant classes. In: S. Brown & S. Cleave (Eds) *Four-Year-olds in School: policy and practice*. Slough: NFER/SCDC.

Siraj-Blatchford, I., Sylva, K., Muttock, S., Golden, R. & Bell, D. (2002) *Researching Effective Pedagogy in the Early Years*, Research Report 356. London: DfES.

Siraj-Blatchford, I., Sylva, K., Muttock, S., Golden, R. & Bell, D. (2006) *Monitoring and Evaluation of the Effective Implementation of the Foundation Phase Project Across Wales*. Cardiff: Welsh National Assembly.

Smith, S. (1990) The riskiness of the playground. *Journal of Educational Thought*, 24(2).

Smith, S. (1998) *Risk and our Pedagogical Relation to Children*. New York: State University of New York Press.

Smith, P. K. (2005) Physical activity and rough-and-tumble play. In: J. Moyles (Ed.) *The Excellence of Play*, 2nd edn. Maidenhead: Open University Press.

Sobel, D. (1990) A place in the world: adults' memories of childhood's special places. *Children's Environments Quarterly*, 7(4), 5–12.

Sobel, D. (1996) *Beyond Ecophobia. Reclaiming the Heart in Nature Education*. Great Barrington: Orion Society.

Sobel, D. (2002) *Children's Special Places. Exploring the role of Dens, Forts and Bush Houses in Middle Childhood*. Detroit: Wayne State University.

Spiegal, B (2007) *Negligence, Play and Risk: legal opinion*. Available at: www.playlink.org.uk/articles (accessed 8 February 2007).

Stephenson, A. (2002) Opening up the outdoors: exploring the relationship between the indoor and the outdoor environment of a centre. *Early Childhood Education Research*, 10, 29–38.

Stephenson, A. (2003) Physical risk taking: dangerous or endangered? *Early Years*, 23(1), 35–43.

Stine, S. (1997) *Landscapes for Learning: creating outdoor environments for children and youth*. New York: John Wiley & Sons Inc.

Straw, H. (1990) The nursery garden. *Early Child Development and Care*, 57, 109–119.

Suantah, M. (2005) Unpublished student essay, Roehampton University, London.

Sylva, K., Roy, C. & Painter, M. (1980) *Childwatching at Playgroup and Nursery School*. London: Grant McIntyre.

Tai, L., Taylor Haque, M., McLlellan, G. & Jordan Knight, E. (2006) *Designing Environments for Children. Landscaping Schoolyards, Gardens and Playgrounds*. New York: McGraw-Hill.

The Children's Society (2003) *Grumpy Adults*. London: Children's Society.

Titman, W. (1994) *Special Places; Special People: the hidden curriculum of the school grounds*. Godalming: Learning Through Landscapes.

Tizard, B. & Hughes, M. (1984) *Young Children Learning: talking and thinking at home and at school*. London: Fontana Paperbacks.

Tovey, H. (1994) *Young Children's Learning: a re-appraisal of sand and water play*. Unpublished MA Dissertation, Roehampton Institute, University of Surrey.

Tovey, H. (2006) *The Dangers of Safety: perceptions of risk in outdoor play*, paper presented at ROERCE Conference, Roehampton University London, 13 December 2005.

Trawick Smith, J. (1998a) School based play and social interactions: opportunities and limitations. In: P. D. Fromberg & D. Bergen (Eds)

Play from Birth to Twelve and Beyond: contexts, perspectives and meanings. New York: Garland Publishing.

Trawick Smith, J. (1998b) A qualitative analysis of metaplay in the preschool years. *Early Childhood Research Quarterly*, 13(3), 433–452.

Trevarthen, C. (1995) The child's need to learn a culture. *Children and Society*, 9, 5–19.

Tuan, Y. F. (1977) *Space and Place: the perspective of experience.* Minneapolis: University of Minnesota Press.

Underdown, A. (2007) *Young Children's Health and Well-being.* Maidenhead: Open University Press.

Valentine, G. & McKendrick, J. (1997) Children's outdoor play: exploring parental concerns about children's safety and the changing nature of childhood. *Geoforum*, 28, 219–235.

Van der Eyken, W. (1975) *Adventures in Education.* Harmondsworth: Pelican.

Vechi, V. (1998) What kind of space for living well in school? In: C. Ceppi & M. Zini (Eds) *Children, Spaces and Relations: metaproject for an environment for young children.* Milan: Domus Academy & Reggio Children.

Vygotsky, L. (1978) *Mind in Society.* Cambridge: Harvard University Press.

Waller, T. (2006) 'Don't Come Too Close to My Octopus Tree': recording and evaluating young children's perspectives on outdoor learning. *Children, Youth and Environments*, 16(2), 75–104.

Wells, G. (1986) *The Meaning Makers: children learning language and using language to learn.* Sevenoaks: Hodder & Stoughton.

Whitehead, M. (1995) Nonsense rhyme and word play in young children. In: R. Beard (Ed.) *Rhyme, Reading and Writing.* London: Hodder & Stoughton.

Williams-Siegfredsen, J. (2005) Run the risk. *Nursery World*, 4 August.

Williams, G. M. (1994) Talk on the climbing frame. *Early Child Development and Care*, 102, 81–89.

Wood, D. (1993) Ground to stand on: some notes on kids' dirt play. *Children's Environments*, 10, 3–18.

INDEX

/

Related books from Open University Press
Purchase from www.openup.co.uk or order through your
local bookseller

KEY TIMES
A FRAMEWORK FOR DEVELOPING HIGH QUALITY
PROVISION FOR CHILDREN FROM BIRTH TO THREE

Julia Manning-Morton and Maggie Thorp

This training resource pack supports practitioners working with children
from birth to three years in developing high quality provision and practice,
in order to meet the needs of our youngest children more effectively. The
pack:

- Explains the key characteristics of children from birth to three in an
  accessible way
- Enables practitioners to ground their practice in what is important to
  babies and toddlers
- Encourages practitioners to reflect on and review the quality of their
  provision and extend their knowledge
- Affirms and builds on practitioners' existing knowledge

Developed in partnership with skilled practitioners, the pack covers key
aspects of research and theory and includes examples of good practice and
observations of children from birth to three. The video illustrates instances
of good practice and provides material for practitioners to analyse and
discuss as a precursor to evaluating their own settings.

*Key Times: A Framework for Developing High Quality Provision for Children
from Birth to Three* is an essential resource for anyone working with, or
training others to work with, children from birth to three.

Contents
Acknowledgements – Foreword – Introduction – **Section one: The key characteristics of children from birth to three** *– Close relationships – Physical and
emotional dependency – Mobility, dexterity and independence – A Sense of self
– Social relationships – Communication – Curiosity and exploration – Creating,
imagining and representing –* **Section two: Key aspects of practice** *– Leading
and managing provision for children from birth to three - Key working and the
key person approach – Settling new children into the setting – Organising
routine times as prime times of the day – Guiding the behaviour of children
from birth to three – Diversity and children from birth to three – The role of the
practitioner in the play of children from birth to three – Observing and recording the interests, development and learning of children from birth to three –
Play opportunities for children from birth to three – Planning provision for
children from birth to three – References and further reading – Appendix: The
key times project.*

2006   218pp
978–0–335–21765–6 (3 ring binder with CD-ROM)

ETHICAL RESEARCH WITH CHILDREN

Edited by Ann Farrell

This book focuses on doing ethical research with children in today's climate of increased globalization, surveillance and awareness of children as competent research participants. It covers a range of conceptual, methodological and procedural issues, and provides a framework for doing ethical research with children.

Written by international experts in the fields of early childhood research and ethics, this book supports students, practitioner-researchers and research gatekeepers with resources on how to conduct and evaluate ethical research with children. The contributors:

- Use key examples of cutting-edge research from a range of countries to examine research ethics with children and those around them
- Provide strategies for planning, conducting and evaluating research in an ethical way
- Explore theoretical approaches to children and childhood that are relevant to ethical research

Ethical Research with Children is key reading for students in childhood studies, teacher education, public health, nursing, human services, legal studies, psychology and social sciences, as well as practitioner-researchers in these fields.

Contents
Contributors – Ethics and research with children – Research ethics in a culture of risk – Designing ethical research with children – Ethical research with very young children – Opening the research conversation – Researching sensitive issues – Restorative research partnerships in indigenous communities – Ethical inclusion of children with disabilities in research – Transforming research ethics: Choices and challenges of researching with children – Ethical aspects of power in research with children – Researching communities: Towards beneficence – Ethical issues in collaborative research with children – New times in ethical research with children – New possibilities for ethical research with children.

2005   200pp
978–0–335–21650–5 (Paperback)   978–0–335–21651–2 (Hardback)

THE EXCELLENCE OF PLAY
SECOND EDITION

Janet Moyles (ed)

The second edition of this bestselling book encapsulates all the many changes that have taken place in early childhood in the last ten years. Whilst retaining its original message of the vital importance of play as a tool for learning and teaching for children and practitioners, it consolidates this further with current evidence from research and practice and links the most effective practice with the implementation of recent policies.

New contributions for the second edition include:

- Children as social and active agents in their own play
- Practitioners' roles in play and adults' enabling of play
- Play and links with Foundation Stage and FS Profile/legislation and policy
- KS1 links (and beyond)
- Birth to three matters
- Outdoor and physical play, including rough and tumble
- Gender differences
- Play and observation/assessment
- Special Educational Needs and play
- Parents' perspectives on play
- Child development links and play

The importance of curriculum and assessment is retained and extended. *The Excellence of Play* supports all those who work in early childhood education and care in developing and implementing the highest quality play experiences for children from birth to middle childhood. All the contributors are experts in their fields and all are passionate about the excellence of play. The book will stimulate and inform the ongoing debate about play through its powerful – and ongoing argument – that 'a curriculum which sanctions and utilizes play is more likely to provide well-balanced citizens of the future as well as happier and more learned children in the present'.

Contributors
Lesley Abbott, Ann Langston, Sian Adams, Angela Anning, Pat Broadhead, Tina Bruce, Tricia David, Sacha Powell, Bernadette Duffy, Hilary Fabian, Aline-Wendy Dunlop, Rose Griffiths, Nigel Hall, Stephanie Harding, Jane Hislama, Alan Howe, Dan Davies, Neil Kitson, Theodora Papatheodorou, Linda Pound, Peter Smith, David Whitebread, Helen Jameson.

Contents
Introduction – Play and curriculum – Birth to three matters and play – Supporting creativity/identity – Play and SENPlay, language and gender – Impact of play on storytelling – Play, literacy and the teacher – Role play – Outdoor play – Physical and rough and tumble play – Play and Science/Technology – Playing Music – Art in the early years – Mathematics and Play – Play in transitions – Play and different cultures – Reflecting on PlayPlay, the universe and everything – Afterword

c.288pp   0 335 21757 5 (Paperback)   0 335 21758 3 (Hardback)